A LITERARY READER

The
Harlem
Renaissance

Compiled by: Karen Kuehner, Glenview, Illinois

Cover photograph: Langston Hughes, ca. 1920s/© CORBIS

Printed in China

ISBN-13: 978-0-618-04815-1
ISBN-10: 0-618-04815-4

9 10 11 12 DSC 09 08

Table of Contents

PART II: STRUGGLING WITH INJUSTICE

Essay
Returning Soldiers
by W. E. B. DuBois

The most influential African-American writer of the twentieth century urges black World War I veterans to fight "the forces of hell" in the United States in this editorial from The Crisis, the official publication of the NAACP.

Poem
If We Must Die
by Claude McKay

The first major poet of the Harlem Renaissance responds to the race riots that followed the end of World War I.

Poem
Strong Men
by Sterling A. Brown

The folk poet Brown summarizes white injustices and the indomitable spirit of the black race.

Poem
Yet Do I Marvel
by Countee Cullen

A gifted writer muses on classical themes and marvels that God made him a poet.

Poem
A Black Man Talks of Reaping
by Arna Bontemps

The poet gives voice to black tenant farmers.

Short Story
Sanctuary
by Nella Larsen

Annie Poole hides Jim Hammer from the sheriff in a moving story about her choice between two injustices.

Photo Album: Asserting Freedom

PART III: BEING AN INDIVIDUAL

PART IV: DISCOVERING HERITAGE

PART V: REMEMBERING HARLEM

Throughout the reader, vocabulary words appear in boldface type and are footnoted. Specialized or technical words and phrases appear in lightface type and are footnoted.

Celebrating
Harlem

The Renaissance

BY NIKKI GIOVANNI

In the introduction to her book Shimmy Shimmy Shimmy Like My Sister Kate: Looking at the Harlem Renaissance through Poems, *the popular African-American poet Nikki Giovanni (1943–   ) explains what this movement in the arts means to her. She defines* renaissance *and explains why she thinks it is an appropriate term for the movement.*

"Renaissance" is actually a very unusual term to use for the flowering of the arts in Harlem between 1917 and 1935. To say there is a *renaissance* is to say that there is a *re*birth or a *re*flowering, and there would be certainly those who would question, well, where was the original flowering? If you go back to 1619, with Africans landing in Virginia as slaves, and coming through that kind of wilderness, where would the flowering be? And yet if one would choose to be cosmic—I choose always to be cosmic—you would say that there was a **divine intervention**[1] that wanted to put African people in America.

If we are going to be cosmic, we would have to say there were golden ages in Africa. If that was the case, then the Harlem Renaissance was connected to the great kingdoms of Songhay and Mali, and to the kingdoms of Egypt, but it would also be connected to the great kingdoms that came out of the Sudan, that came out of Zimbabwe—all of these great flowerings throughout history. So the Harlem Renaissance was the first American flowering of the black people.

I'm not a scholar. I'm not trying to approach this book on a scholarly basis. I don't want somebody calling me up and saying, "Well, good Lord, you can't possibly suggest a connection from ancient Africa to modern America." Yet I'm feeling there is a link. And I think connection is important, because if we recognize the African connection, then we can also see a kinship with the other renaissances—the Greek, and Roman, the Italian, even the British. So to see a link is not to exclude. . . .

I can't help but think that whoever was around when Michelangelo[2] was painting, or Leonardo da Vinci,[3] knew that something was in the air. When Dante[4] wrote *The Divine Comedy*, there were many people who couldn't read Italian. The people in whose language he wrote it were essentially **illiterate**,[5] but they knew something had happened. Same with the Harlem Renaissance: everybody knew something had happened. They may not have been

---

[1] **divine intervention**—act of God in human affairs.

[2] Michelangelo—Michelangelo Buonarroti (1475–1564), Italian Renaissance sculptor, painter, architect, and poet whose works include the paintings on the ceiling of the Sistine Chapel in Rome.

[3] Leonardo da Vinci—(1452–1519) Italian Renaissance painter, engineer, musician, and scientist whose works include *The Last Supper*.

[4] Dante—Dante Durante Alighieri (1265–1321) Italian poet known especially for *The Divine Comedy*, a philosophical poem recounting an imaginary journey through Hell, Purgatory, and Paradise. It is considered a masterpiece of world literature.

[5] **illiterate**—unable to read and write.

able to always tell you what, and it probably was annoying that there were so many places right there in Harlem where black patrons were not welcome. But they knew.

The Renaissance was a great flowering. It was a people deciding that we will wage war with images. We will wage war with creativity, with words, with our souls. We will not stoop to be what you think we are, nor will we stoop to be what you are trying to make us. We are going, in the words of the old spiritual, "to plant our feet on higher ground." That's what is outstanding about this period.

QUESTIONS TO CONSIDER

1. Why does Giovanni think that *renaissance* is an unusual term to use for the flowering of the arts in Harlem between 1917 and 1935?

2. Which events in Africa does Giovanni link to the Harlem Renaissance? Why?

3. What does Giovanni suggest that the people of the Harlem Renaissance are warring against?

from

Black Manhattan

BY JAMES WELDON JOHNSON

*James Weldon Johnson (1871–1938) excelled as an educator,
writer, diplomat, and social activist. He taught the children of
former slaves in a school in rural Georgia; he served as school
principal in his hometown of Jacksonville, Florida; and he ended his
career as the Spence Chair of Creative Literature at Fisk University.
In between, he was a successful writer of poems and songs for
Broadway shows, a member of the American foreign service, and
an activist for the rights of African Americans. His "Lift Ev'ry Voice
and Sing" is known as the "Negro National Anthem." In the diplo-
matic corps, he served as consul in both Venezuela and Nicaragua.
In 1916 he was asked to become the national organizer of the
National Association for the Advancement of Colored People
(NAACP) and later he became the first African American to
head the organization. In the following essay from his book*
Black Manhattan *(1930), he describes Harlem, the New York
City neighborhood that was home to the Harlem Renaissance.*

If you ride northward the length of Manhattan Island, going through Central Park and coming out on Seventh Avenue or Lenox Avenue at One Hundred and Tenth Street, you cannot escape being struck by the sudden change in the character of the people you see. In the middle and lower parts of the city you have, perhaps, noted Negro faces here and there; but when you emerge from the Park, you see them everywhere, and as you go up either of these two great arteries[1] leading out from the city to the north, you see more and more Negroes, walking in the streets, looking from the windows, trading in the shops, eating in the restaurants, going in and coming out of the theaters, until, nearing One Hundred and Thirty-fifth Street, ninety per cent of the people you see, including the traffic officers, are Negroes. And it is not until you cross the Harlem River that the population whitens again, which it does as suddenly as it began to darken at One Hundred and Tenth Street. You have been having an outside glimpse of Harlem, the Negro metropolis.

In nearly every city in the country the Negro section is a nest or several nests situated somewhere on the borders; it is a section one must "go out to." In New York it is entirely different. Negro Harlem is situated in the heart of Manhattan and covers one of the most beautiful and healthful sites in the whole city. It is not a fringe, it is not a slum, nor is it a "quarter" consisting of dilapidated tenements.[2] It is a section of new-law apartment houses[3] and handsome dwellings, with streets as well paved, as well lighted, and as well kept as in any other part of the city. Three main highways lead into and out from upper Manhattan, and two of them run straight through Harlem. So Harlem is not a section that one "goes out to," but a section that one goes through. . . .

---

[1] arteries—main roads.

[2] dilapidated tenements—broken-down, shabby apartment buildings.

[3] new-law apartment houses—modern, up-to-date homes.

Roughly drawn, the boundaries of Harlem are: One Hundred and Tenth Street on the south; on the east, Lenox Avenue to One Hundred and Twenty-sixth Street, then Lexington Avenue to the Harlem River, and the Harlem River on the east and north to a point where it passes the Polo Grounds just above One Hundred and Fifty-fifth Street; on the west, Eighth Avenue to One Hundred and Sixteenth Street, then St. Nicholas Avenue up to a **juncture**[4] with the Harlem River at the Polo Grounds. To the east of the Lenox Avenue boundary there are a score of blocks of mixed colored and white population; and to the west of the Eighth Avenue boundary there is a solid Negro border, two blocks wide, from One Hundred and Sixteenth Street to One Hundred and Twenty-fifth Street. The heights north from One Hundred and Forty-fifth Street, known as Coogan's Bluff, are solidly black. Within this area of less than two square miles live more than two hundred thousand Negroes, more to the square acre than in any other place on earth.

This city within a city, in these larger proportions, is actually a development of the last fifteen years. The **trek**[5] to Harlem began when the West Fifty-third Street center had reached its utmost development; that is, early in the decade 1900–10. The move to West Fifty-third Street had been the result of the opportunity to get into better houses; and the move to Harlem was due to the same urge. In fact, Harlem offered the colored people the first chance in their entire history in New York to live in modern apartment houses. West Fifty-third Street was superior to anything they had ever enjoyed; and there they were, for the most part, making private dwellings serve the purpose of apartments, housing several families in each house. The move to Harlem, in the beginning and for a long time, was fathered and engineered by Philip A. Payton, a colored man in the real-estate business. But

---

[4] **juncture**—connection; place where two points meet.
[5] **trek**—migration.

this was more than a matter of mere business with Mr. Payton; the matter of better and still better housing for colored people in New York became the dominating idea of his life, and he worked on it as long as he lived. . . .

Harlem had been overbuilt with new apartment houses. It was far uptown, and the only rapid transportation was the elevated[6] running up Eighth Avenue—the Lenox Avenue Subway had not yet been built. This left the people on Lenox Avenue and to the east with only the electric street-cars convenient. So landlords were finding it hard to fill their houses on that side of the section. Mr. Payton approached several of these landlords with the proposal to fill their empty houses with colored tenants and keep them filled. Economic necessity usually discounts race prejudice—or any other kind of prejudice—as much as ninety per cent, sometimes a hundred; so the landlords with empty houses whom Mr. Payton approached accepted his proposal, and one or two houses on One Hundred and Thirty-fourth Street were taken over and filled with colored tenants. Gradually other houses were filled. . . .

Colored people not only continued to move into apartments outside the zone east of Lenox Avenue, but began to purchase the fine private houses between Lenox and Seventh. Then, in the eyes of the whites who were **antagonistic**,[7] the whole movement took on the aspect of an "invasion"—an invasion of both their economic and their social rights. . . . The presence of a single colored family in a block, regardless of the fact that they might be well-bred people, with sufficient means to buy their new home, was a signal for **precipitate**[8] flight. The stampeded whites actually deserted house after house and block after block. Then prices dropped; they dropped lower than the

---

[6] elevated—elevated train; railway that operates on a raised structure to permit passage beneath it.

[7] **antagonistic**—hostile; in opposition to.

[8] **precipitate**—sudden; hasty; impetuous.

bottom, and such colored people as were able took advantage of these prices and bought. Some of the banks and lending companies that were compelled to take over deserted houses for the mortgages they held refused for a time to either sell or rent them to Negroes. Instead, they proposed themselves to bear the carrying charges and hold them vacant for what they evidently hoped would be a temporary period. Prices continued to drop. And this was the property situation in Harlem at the outbreak of the World War in Europe.

With the outbreak of the war there came a sudden change. One of the first effects of the war was to draw thousands of aliens out of this country back to their native lands to join the colors.[9] Naturally, there was also an almost total **cessation**[10] of immigration. Moreover, the United States was almost immediately called upon to furnish munitions and supplies of all kinds to the warring countries. The result of these converging causes was an unprecedented shortage of labor and a demand that was **imperative**.[11] From whence could the necessary supply be drawn? There was only one source, and that was the reservoir of black labor in the South. And it was at once drawn on to fill the existing vacuum in the great industries of the North. Every available method was used to get these black hands, the most effective being the sending of labor agents into the South, who dealt directly with the Negroes, arranged for their transportation, and shipped them north, often in single **consignments**[12] running high up into the hundreds. I witnessed the sending north from a Southern city in one day a crowd estimated at twenty-five hundred. They were shipped on a train run in three sections, packed in day coaches, with

---

[9] colors—flags; Johnson refers to immigrants who returned home during World War I to fight in their countries' armed forces.

[10] **cessation**—end; stop.

[11] **imperative**—urgent.

[12] **consignments**—shipments, usually of merchandise that is paid for after it has been sold, or, in this case, hired.

all their baggage and other **impedimenta**.[13] The exodus
was on, and migrants came north in thousands, tens of
thousands, hundreds of thousands—from the docks of
Norfolk, Savannah, Jacksonville, Tampa, Mobile, New
Orleans, and Galveston; from the cotton-fields of
Mississippi, and the coal-mines and steel-mills of
Alabama and Tennessee; from workshops and wash-tubs
and brick-yards and kitchens they came, until the number, by conservative estimate, went well over the million
and a half mark. For the Negroes of the South this was
the happy blending of desire with opportunity.

It could not be otherwise in such a wholesale migration then that many who came were ignorant, inefficient,
and worthless, and that there was also a proportion of
downright criminals. But industry was in no position to
be **fastidious**;[14] it was glad to take what it could get. It was
not until the return of more normal conditions that the
process of elimination of the incapable and the unfit set in.
Meanwhile, in these new fields, the Negro was acquiring
all sorts of divergent reputations for capability. In some
places he was rated A1 and in others N.G.,[15] and in vary-
ing degrees between these two extremes. The explanation,
of course, is that different places had secured different
kinds of Negroes. On the whole, New York was more fortunate in the migrants she got than were some of the large
cities. Most of the industries in the manufacturing cities of
the Middle West—except the steel-mills, which drew
largely on the skilled and semi-skilled labor from the
mills of Alabama and Tennessee—received migrants
from the cotton-raising regions of the lower Mississippi
Valley, from the rural, even the backwoods, districts,
Negroes who were unused to city life or anything bearing
a resemblance to modern industry. On the other hand,
New York drew most of her migrants from cities and

---

[13] **impedimenta**—equipment and supplies that slow rapid movement.
[14] **fastidious**—overly particular; difficult to satisfy.
[15] N.G.—No Good.

towns of the Atlantic seaboard states, Negroes who were far better prepared to adapt themselves to life and industry in a great city. Nor did all of New York's Negro migrants come from the South. The opportunity for Negro labor exerted a pull that reached down to the Negroes of the West Indies, and many of them came, most of them directly to New York. Those from the British West Indies average high in intelligence and efficiency. There is practically no illiteracy among them, and many have a sound English common school education. They are characteristically sober minded and have something of a genius for business, differing almost totally, in these respects, from the average rural Negro of the South. Those from the British possessions constitute the great majority of the West Indians in New York; but there is also a large number who are Spanish-speaking and a considerable, though smaller, number who are French-speaking. The total West Indian population of Harlem is approximately fifty thousand.

With thousands of Negroes pouring into Harlem month by month, two things happened: first, a sheer physical pressure for room was set up that was irresistible; second, old residents and new comers got work as fast as they could take it, at wages never dreamed of, so there was now plenty of money for renting and buying. And the Negro in Harlem did, contrary to all the **burlesque**[16] notions about what Negroes do when they get hold of money, take advantage of the low prices of property and begin to buy. Buying property became a contagious fever. It became a part of the gospel preached in the churches. It seems that generations of the experience of an extremely **precarious**[17] foothold on the land of Manhattan Island flared up into a conscious determination never to let that condition return. So they turned the

---

16 **burlesque**—exaggerated; distorted.
17 **precarious**—insecure.

money from their new-found prosperity into property. . . . Twenty years ago barely a half-dozen colored individuals owned land on Manhattan. Down to fifteen years ago the amount that Negroes had acquired in Harlem was by comparison **negligible**.[18] Today a very large part of the property in Harlem occupied by Negroes is owned by Negroes.

---

[18] **negligible**—not significant enough to be worth considering.

QUESTIONS TO CONSIDER

1. What factors led to Harlem's becoming a center for African Americans?

2. What adjectives would you use to describe Johnson's emotions toward the growth of Harlem?

3. How, in your opinion, would the background of the people who came into Harlem contribute to the artistic expression that developed there?

Conversation with James P. Johnson

BY TOM DAVIN

The Harlem Renaissance is primarily associated with literature, but many of its writers and artists found inspiration in the popular music of the twenties: jazz. Nowhere was jazz better, or hotter, than in the clubs of Harlem. Although pianist/composer James P. Johnson (1894–1955) is not as well known today as his unofficial students Fats Waller and Duke Ellington, he is regarded as the founder of the "stride" style of jazz piano. The stride style emphasizes both rhythmic variations and the harmonies that occur when a pianist plays two or more notes simultaneously. Interviewed in 1953, two years before his death, Johnson describes the style, both personal and musical, of some other Harlem jazz pianists.

Q. What was Willie (The Lion) Smith like in his young days?

A. Willie Smith was one of the sharpest ticklers[1] I ever met—and I met most of them. When we first met in

---

[1] ticklers—piano players, so-called because their fingers seemed to "tickle" the keys.

Newark, he wasn't called Willie The Lion—he got that nickname after his terrific fighting record overseas during World War I. He was a fine dresser, very careful about the cut of his clothes and a fine dancer, too, in addition to his great playing. All of us used to be proud of our dancing—Louis Armstrong, for instance, was considered the finest dancer among the musicians. It made for attitude and stance when you walked into a place, and made you strong with the gals. When Willie Smith walked into a place, his every move was a picture.

Q. You mean he would make a **studied**[2] entrance, like a theatrical star?

A. Yes; every move we made was studied, practiced, and developed just like it was a complicated piano piece.

Q. What would such an entrance be like?

A. When a real smart tickler would enter a place, say in winter, he'd leave his overcoat on and keep his hat on, too. We used to wear military overcoats or what was called a Peddock Coat, like a coachman's; a blue double-breasted, fitted to the waist and with long skirts. We'd wear a light pearl-gray Fulton or Homburg[3] hat with three buttons or eyelets on the side, set at a rakish angle over on the side of the head. Then a white silk muffler and a white silk handkerchief in the overcoat's breast pocket. Some carried a gold-headed cane, or if they were wearing a cutaway,[4] a silver-headed cane. A couple of fellows used to wear Inverness capes,[5] which were in style in white society then.

Many fellows had their overcoats lined with the same material as the outside—they even had their suits made that way. Pawnbrokers, special ones, would give

---

[2] **studied**—carefully contrived; calculated.

[3] Fulton or Homburg—felt hat with a slightly turned-up brim and a soft crown dented lengthwise.

[4] cutaway—man's formal coat whose front edges sloped diagonally from the waist and formed tails in the back.

[5] Inverness capes—hip-length capes with round collars, often attached to coats of the same fabric.

you twenty or twenty-five dollars on such a suit or overcoat. They knew what it was made of. A fellow belittling another would be able to say: "G'wan, the inside of my coat would make you a suit."

But to go back . . . when you came into a place you had a three-way play. You never took your overcoat or hat off until you were at the piano. First you laid your cane on the music rack. Then you took off your overcoat, folded it and put it on the piano, with the lining showing.

You then took off your hat before the audience. Each tickler had his own gesture for removing his hat with a little flourish; that was part of his attitude, too. You took out your silk handkerchief, shook it out and dusted off the piano stool.

Now, with your coat off, the audience could admire your full-back or box-back suit, cut with very square shoulders. The pants had about fourteen-inch cuffs and broidered clocks.[6]

Full-back coats were always single-breasted, to show your gold watch fob and chain. Some ticklers wore a horseshoe tiepin in a strong single-colored tie and a gray shirt with black pencil stripes.

We all wore French, Shriner & Urner or Hanan straight or French last shoes with very pointed toes, or patent-leather turnup toes, in very narrow sizes. For instance, if you had a size 7 foot, you'd wear an 8½ shoe on a very narrow last.[7] They cost from twelve to eighteen dollars a pair.

If you had an expensive suit made, you'd have the tailor take a piece of cloth and give it to you, so that you could have either spats[8] or button cloth-tops for your shoes to match the suit.

Some sharp men would have a suit and overcoat made of the same bolt of cloth. Then they'd take another

---

[6] broidered clocks—vertical, embroidered decorations on or near a seam.

[7] last—foot-shaped form.

[8] spats—cloth or leather coverings for shoes.

piece of the same goods and have a three-button Homburg made out of it. This was only done with solid-color cloth—tweeds or plaids were not in good taste for formal hats. . . .

Of course each tickler had his own style of appearance. I used to study them carefully and copy those attitudes that appealed to me.

There was a fellow named Fred Tunstall. . . . He was a real dandy. I remember he had a Norfolk coat with eighty-two pleats in the back. When he sat down to the piano, he'd slump a little in a half hunch, and those pleats would fan out real pretty. That coat was long and flared at the waist. It had a very short belt sewn on the back. His pants were very tight.

He had a long neck, so he wore a high, stiff collar that came up under his chin with a purple tie. A silk handkerchief was always draped very carefully in his breast pocket. His side view was very striking.

Tunstall was very careful about his hair, which was ordinary, but he used lots of **pomade**.[9] His favorite shoes were patent-leather turnups.

His playing was fair, but he had the reputation of being one of our most elegant dressers. He had thirty-five suits of clothes—blacks, grays, brown pin stripes, oxfords, pepper and salts.

Some men would wear a big diamond ring on their pinky, the right-hand one, which would flash in the treble[10] passages. Gold teeth were in style, and a real sharp effect was to have a diamond set on one tooth. One fellow went further and had diamonds set in the teeth of his toy Boston bulldog. . . .

Q. Where did these styles come from, the South?

A. No, we saw them right here in New York City. They were all copied from the styles of the rich whites.

---

[9] **pomade**—ointment used to style hair.

[10] treble—high notes, notes above middle C, which are played on the piano with the right hand.

Most of the society folks had colored **valets**[11] and some of them would give their old clothes to their valets and household help.

Then we'd see rich people at society **gigs**[12] in the big hotels where they had Clef Club[13] bands for their dances. So we wanted to dress good, copied them and made improvements.

Q. Please tell me more about the great ticklers' styles.

A. As I was saying, when I was a young fellow, I was very much impressed with such manners. I didn't know much about style, but I wanted to learn. I didn't want to be a punk all my life.

In the sporting world of gamblers, hustlers and ticklers, the lowest rank is called a punk. He's nothing. He doesn't have any sense; he doesn't know anything about life or the school of the smart world. He doesn't even know how to act in public. You had to have an attitude, a style of behaving that was your personal, professional trade-mark. . . .

I've seen Jelly Roll Morton, who had a great attitude, approach a piano. He would take his overcoat off. It had a special lining that would catch everybody's eye. So he would turn it inside out and, instead of folding it, he would lay it lengthwise along the top of the upright piano. He would do this very slowly, very carefully and very solemnly as if the coat was worth a fortune and had to be handled very tenderly.

Then he'd take a big silk handkerchief, shake it out to show it off properly, and dust off the stool. He'd sit down then, hit his special chord (every tickler had his special trade-mark chord, like a **signal**) and he'd be gone! The first **rag**[14] he'd play was always a spirited one to astound the audience.

---

[11] **valets**—servants; personal assistants.

[12] **gigs**—jobs.

[13] Clef Club—Harlem nightclub noted for its music.

[14] rag—song in ragtime, an early form of jazz.

Other players would start off by sitting down, wait for the audience to quiet down and then strike their chord, holding it with the pedal to make it ring.

Then they'd do a run up and down the piano—a scale or **arpeggios**[15]—or if they were real good they might play a set of **modulations**,[16] very offhand, as if there was nothing to it. They'd look around idly to see if they knew any chicks near the piano. If they saw somebody, they'd start a light conversation about the theater, the races or social doings—light chat. At this time, they'd drift into a rag, any kind of pretty stuff, but without tempo, particularly without tempo. Some ticklers would sit sideways to the piano, cross their legs and go on chatting with friends near by. It took a lot of practice to play this way, while talking and with your head and body turned.

Then, without stopping the smart talk or turning back to the piano, he'd *attack* without any warning, smashing right into the regular beat of the piece. That would knock them dead.

---

[15] **arpeggios**—notes of multiple chords played singly, not simultaneously.

[16] **modulations**—succession of chords that move from one key to another.

QUESTIONS TO CONSIDER

1. What attributes did a successful tickler need?

2. Why do you think clothes were so important to these musicians?

3. What effect might these musicians have had on their audiences?

4. Which musicians today have a distinctive style or attitude?

Jazzonia

BY LANGSTON HUGHES

The poet and writer who most helped define the Harlem Renaissance is Langston Hughes (1902–1967). Shortly after Hughes was born, his father went to Mexico and became a successful industrialist. When Hughes was nineteen, his father agreed to send him to New York, provided he study engineering at Columbia University. Hughes later wrote, "I was in love with Harlem long before I got there." A keen observer of both sights and sounds, Hughes was inspired by the poet Carl Sandburg, whom he called his "guiding star," to replicate the rhythms and variations of jazz in his poetry. In "Jazzonia," from The Weary Blues, *published in 1926, Hughes combines his interest in pop music with knowledge of his racial past.*

Oh, silver tree!
Oh, shining rivers of the soul!

In a Harlem **cabaret**[1]
Six long-headed jazzers[2] play.
A dancing girl whose eyes are bold
Lifts high a dress of silken gold.
Oh, singing tree!
Oh, shining rivers of the soul!

Were Eve's eyes
In the first garden
Just a bit too bold?
Was Cleopatra gorgeous
In a gown of gold?

Oh, shining tree!
Oh, silver rivers of the soul!

In a whirling cabaret
Six long-headed jazzers play.

---

[1] **cabaret**—restaurant; nightclub.
[2] jazzers—jazz musicians.

QUESTIONS TO CONSIDER

1. How would you describe Hughes's attitude toward his subject?

2. Why does Hughes refer to Eve and Cleopatra? To the tree and the river?

3. In what ways does Hughes's poem echo the rhythms of jazz?

Miss Cynthie

BY RUDOLPH FISHER

Some cultural historians consider Rudolph Fisher (1897–1934) the most intellectually gifted of all the Harlem Renaissance figures. Not only was Fisher a musical composer, essayist, and fiction writer, but he was also a medical doctor who had specialized in radiology before opening a private practice in Harlem in 1927. In "Miss Cynthie," Fisher portrays the effect of life in Harlem on an unsophisticated but righteous southern woman.

For the first time in her life somebody had called her "madam."

She had been standing, bewildered but unafraid, while innumerable Red Caps[1] appropriated piece after piece of the baggage arrayed on the platform. Neither her brief seventy years' journey through life nor her long two days' travel northward had dimmed the live brightness of her eyes, which, for all their bewilderment, had

---

[1] Red Caps—porters who carry luggage to and from trains and taxis.

accurately selected her own treasures out of the row of luggage and guarded them **vigilantly**.[2]

"These yours, madam?"

The biggest Red Cap of all was smiling at her. He looked for all the world like Doc Crinshaw's oldest son back home. Her little brown face relaxed; she smiled back at him.

"They got to be. You all done took all the others."

He laughed aloud. Then—"Carry 'em in for you?"

She contemplated his bulk. "Reckon you can manage it—puny little feller like you?"

Thereupon they were friends. Still grinning broadly, he surrounded himself with her impedimenta, the enormous brown extension-case on one shoulder, the big straw suitcase in the opposite hand, the carpet-bag under one arm. She herself held fast to the umbrella.

"Always like to have sump'm in my hand when I walk. Can't never tell when you'll run across a snake."

"There aren't any snakes in the city."

"There's snakes everywhere, chile."[3]

They began the tedious hike up the **interminable**[4] platform. She was small and quick. Her carriage was surprisingly erect, her gait astonishingly spry. She said:

"You liked to took my breath back yonder, boy, callin' me 'madam.' Back home everybody call me 'Miss Cynthie.' Even my own chillun.[5] Even their chillun. Black folks, white folks too. 'Miss Cynthie.' Well, when you come up with that 'madam' o' yourn, I say to myself, 'Now, I wonder who that chile's a-grinnin' at? 'Madam' stand for mist'ess o' the house, and I sho' ain' mist'ess o' nothin' in this hyeh New York.'"

"Well, you see, we call everybody 'madam.'"

---

[2] **vigilantly**—carefully; with great attention.

[3] chile—[slang] child.

[4] **interminable**—endless.

[5] chillun—[slang] children.

"Everybody?—Hm." The bright eyes twinkled. "Seem like that'd worry me some—if I was a man."

He acknowledged his slip and observed, "I see this isn't your first trip to New York."

"First trip any place, son. First time I been over fifty mile from Waxhaw.[6] Only travelin' I've done is in my head. Ain' seen many places, but I's seen a **passel**[7] o' people. Reckon places is pretty much alike after people been in 'em awhile."

"Yes, ma'am. I guess that's right."

"You am' no reg'lar bag-toter, is you?"

"Ma'am?"

"You talk too good."

"Well, I only do this in vacation-time. I'm still in school."

"You is. What you aimin' to be?"

"I'm studying medicine."

"You is?" She beamed. "Aimin' to be a doctor, huh? Thank the Lord for that. That's what I always wanted my David to be. My grandchile hyeh in New York He's to meet me hyeh now."

"I bet you'll have a great time."

"Mussn't bet, chile. That's sinful. I tole him 'fo' he left home, I say, 'Son, you the only one o' the chillun what's got a chance to amount to sump'm. Don' th'ow it away. Be a preacher or a doctor. Work yo' way up and don' stop short. If the Lord don' see fit for you to doctor the soul, then doctor the body. If you don' get to be a reg'lar doctor, be a tooth-doctor. If you 'jes' can't make that, be a foot-doctor. And if you don' get that fur, be a undertaker. That's the least you must be. That ain' so bad. Keep you acquainted with the house of the Lord. Always mind the house o' the Lord   whatever you do, do like a church-steeple: aim high and go straight.'"

"Did he get to be a doctor?"

---

[6] Waxhaw—city in North Carolina.

[7] **passel**—parcel, a large quantity or number.

"Don' b'lieve he did. Too late startin', I reckon. But he's done succeeded at sump'm. Mus' be at least a undertaker, 'cause he started sendin' the home-folks money, and he come home las' year dressed like Judge Pettiford's boy what went off to school in Virginia. Wouldn't tell none of us 'zackly what he was doin', but he said he wouldn't never be happy till I come and see for myself. So hyeh I is." Something softened her voice. "His mammy died befo' he knowed her. But he was always sech a good chile—" The something was apprehension. "Hope he *is* a undertaker."

They were mounting a flight of steep stairs leading to an exit-gate, about which clustered a few people still hoping to catch sight of arriving friends. Among these a tall young brown-skinned man in a light grey suit suddenly waved his **panama**[8] and yelled, "Hey, Miss Cynthie!"

Miss Cynthie stopped, looked up, and waved back with a delighted umbrella. The Red Cap's eyes lifted too. His lower jaw sagged.

"Is that your grandson?"

"It sho' is," she said and distanced him for the rest of the climb. The grandson, with an abandonment that superbly ignored onlookers, folded the little woman in an exultant, smothering embrace. As soon as she could, she pushed him off with breathless mock impatience.

"Go 'way, you fool, you. Aimin' to squeeze my soul out my body befo' I can get a look at this place?" She shook herself into the semblance of composure. "Well. You don' look hungry, anyhow."

"Ho-ho! Miss Cynthie in New York! Can y'imagine this? Come on. I'm parked on Eighth Avenue."

The Red Cap delivered the outlandish luggage into a robin's egg blue open **Packard**[9] with scarlet wheels,

---

[8] **panama**—lightweight summer hat made from natural-colored straw.
[9] **Packard**—large, expensive car produced between 1899 and 1958.

accepted the grandson's dollar and smile, and stood watching the car roar away up Eighth Avenue.

Another Red Cap came up. "Got a break, hey, boy?"

"Dave Tappen himself—can you beat that?"

"The old lady hasn't seen the station yet—starin' at him."

"That's not the half of it, bozo. That's Dave Tappen's grandmother. And what do you s'pose she hopes?"

"What?"

"She hopes that Dave has turned out to be a successful undertaker!"

"Undertaker? Undertaker!"

They stared at each other a gaping moment, then doubled up with laughter.

* * *

"Look—through there—that's the Chrysler Building. Oh, hell-elujah! I meant to bring you up Broadway—"

"David—"

"Ma'am?"

"This hyeh wagon yourn?"

"Nobody else's. Sweet buggy, ain't it?"

"David—you ain't turned out to be one of them moonshiners, is you?"

"Moonshiners—? Moon—Ho! No indeed, Miss Cynthie. I got a better racket 'n that."

"Better which?"

"Game. Business Pick-up."

"Tell me, David. What is yo' racket?"

"Can't spill it yet, Miss Cynthie. Rather show you. Tomorrow night you'll know the worst. Can't you make out till tomorrow night?"

"David, you know I always wanted you to be a doctor, even if 'twasn' nothin' but a foot-doctor. The very leas' I wanted you to be was a undertaker."

"Undertaker! Oh, Miss Cynthie!—with my sunny disposition?"

"Then you ain' even a undertaker?"

"Listen, Miss Cynthie. Just forget 'bout what I am for awhile. Just till tomorrow night. I want you to see for yourself. Tellin' you will spoil it. Now stop askin', you hear?—because I'm not answerin'—I'm surprisin' you. And don't expect anybody you meet to tell you. It'll mess up the whole works. Understand? Now give the big city a break. There's the elevated train going up Columbus Avenue. Ain't that hot stuff?"

Miss Cynthie looked. "Humph!" she said. "Tain' half high as that trestle[10] two mile from Waxhaw."

* * *

She thoroughly enjoyed the ride up Central Park West.[11] The stagger lights, the extent of the park, the high, close, kingly dwellings, remarkable because their stoves cooled them in summer as well as heated them in winter, all drew nods of mild interest. But what gave her special delight was not these: it was that David's car so effortlessly sped past the headlong drove of vehicles racing northward.

They stopped for a red light; when they started again their machine leaped forward with a triumphant eagerness that drew from her an unsuppressed, "Hot you, David! That's it!"

He grinned appreciatively. "Why, you're a regular New Yorker already."

"New Yorker nothin'! I done the same thing fifty years ago—befo' I knowed they was a New York."

"What!"

"Deed so. Didn' I use to tell you 'bout my young mare, Betty? Chile, I'd hitch Betty up to yo' grandpa's buggy and pass anything on the road. Betty never

---

10 trestle—braced timber structure that supports a road or railroad track over a depression.

11 Central Park West—north-south boulevard that runs along the west edge of Central Park in Manhattan.

knowed what another horse's dust smelt like. No 'ndeedy. Shuh, boy, this ain' nothin' new to me. Why that brokedown Fo'd you' uncle Jake's got ain' nothin'— nothin' but a sorry mess. Done got so slow I jes' won' ride in it—I declare I'd rather walk. But this hyeh thing, now, this is right nice." She settled back in complete, complacent comfort, and they sped on, swift and silent.

Suddenly she sat erect with abrupt discovery.

"David—well—bless my soul!"

"What's the matter, Miss Cynthie?"

Then he saw what had caught her attention. They were traveling up Seventh Avenue now, and something was miraculously different. Not the road; that was as broad as ever, wide, white gleaming in the sun. Not the houses; they were lofty still, lordly, disdainful, **supercilious**.[12] Not the cars; they continued to race impatiently onward, innumerable, precipitate, **tumultuous**.[13] Something else, something at once obvious and subtle, insistent, pervasive, compelling.

"David—this mus' be Harlem!"

"Good Lord, Miss Cynthie—!"

"Don' use the name of the Lord in vain, David."

"But I mean—gee!—you're no fun at all. You get everything before a guy can tell you."

"You got plenty to tell me, David. But don' nobody need to tell me this. Look a yonder."

Not just a change of complexion. A completely dissimilar atmosphere. Sidewalks teeming with leisurely strollers, at once strangely dark and bright. Boys in white trousers, berets, and green shirts, with slickened black heads and proud swagger. Bareheaded girls in crisp organdie dresses, purple, canary, gay scarlet. And laughter, abandoned strong Negro laughter, some falling full on the ear, some not heard at all, yet sensed the

---

[12] **supercilious**—proud.

[13] **tumultuous**—noisy or disorderly.

warm life-breath of the tireless carnival to which Harlem's heart quickens in summer.

"This is it," admitted David. "Get a good eyeful. Here's One Hundred and Twenty-fifth Street—regular little Broadway. And here's the Alhambra, and up ahead we'll pass the Lafayette."

"What's them?"

"Theaters."

"Theaters? Theaters. Humph! Look, David—is that a colored folks church?" They were passing a fine gray-stone edifice.

"That? Oh. Sure it is. So's this one on this side."

"No! Well, ain' that fine? Splendid big church like that for colored folks."

Taking his cue from this, her first tribute to the city, he said, "You ain't seen nothing yet. Wait a minute."

They swung left through a side-street and turned right on a boulevard. "What do you think o' that?" And he pointed to the quarter-million-dollar St. Mark's.

"That a colored church, too?"

"Tain' no white one. And they built it themselves, you know. Nobody's hand-me-down gift."

She heaved a great happy sigh. "Oh, yes, it was a gift, David. It was a gift from on high." Then, "Look a hyeh—which a one you belong to?"

"Me? Why, I don't belong to any—that is, none o' these. Mine's over in another section. Y'see, mine's Baptist. These are all Methodist. See?"

"M-m. Uh-huh. I see."

They circled a square and slipped into a quiet narrow street overlooking a park, stopping before the tallest of the apartment-houses in the single commanding row.

Alighting, Miss Cynthie gave this imposing structure one sidewise, upward glance, and said, "Y'all live like bees in a hive, don't y'?—I boun' the women does all the work, too." A moment later, "So this is a elevator? Feel like I'm glory-bound sho' nuff."

Along a tiled corridor and into David's apartment. Rooms leading into rooms. Luxurious couches, easy-chairs, a brown-walnut grand piano, gay-shaded floor lamps, panelled walls, deep rugs, treacherous glass-wood floors[14]—and a smiling golden-skinned girl in a gingham house-dress, approaching with outstretched hands.

"This is Ruth, Miss Cynthie."

"Miss Cynthie!" said Ruth.

They clasped hands. "Been wantin' to see David's girl ever since he first wrote us 'bout her."

"Come—here's your room this way. Here's the bath. Get out of your things and get comfy. You must be worn out with the trip."

"Worn out? Worn out? Shuh. How you gon' get worn out on a train? Now if 'twas a horse, maybe, or Jake's no-'count Fo'd—but a train—didn' but one thing bother me on that train."

"What?"

"When the man made them beds down, I jes' couldn' manage to undress same as at home. Why, s'posin' sump'm bus' the train open—where'd you be? Naked as a jay-bird in dew-berry time."

David took in her things and left her to get comfortable. He returned, and Ruth, despite his reassuring embrace, whispered:

"Dave, you can't fool old folks—why don't you go ahead and tell her about yourself? Think of the shock she's going to get—at her age."

David shook his head. "She'll get over the shock if she's there looking on. If we just told her, she'd never understand. We've got to railroad her into it. Then she'll be happy."

"She's nice. But she's got the same ideas as all old folks—"

---

[14] glass-wood floors—wood floors so highly polished they resemble glass.

"Yea—but with her you can change 'em. Specially if everything is really all right. I know her. She's for church and all, but she believes in good times too, if they're right. Why, when I was a kid—" He broke off. "Listen!"

Miss Cynthie's voice came quite distinctly to them, singing a jaunty little rhyme:

"Oh I danced with the gal with the hole in her stockin',
And her toe kep' a-kickin' and her heel kep' a-knockin'—

Come up, Jesse, and get a drink o' gin,
'Cause you near to the heaven as you'll ever get ag'in."

"She taught me that when I wasn't knee-high to a cricket," David said.

Miss Cynthie still sang softly and merrily:

"Then I danced with the gal with the dimple in her cheek,
And if she'd 'a' kep' a-smilin', I'd a' danced for a week—"

"God forgive me," prayed Miss Cynthie as she discovered David's purpose the following night. She let him and Ruth lead her, like an early Christian martyr, into the Lafayette Theater. The blinding glare of the lobby produced a merciful self-anaesthesia, and she entered the sudden dimness of the interior as involuntarily as in a dream—

Attendants outdid each other for Mr. Dave Tappen. She heard him tell them, "Fix us up till we go on," and found herself sitting between Ruth and David in the front row of a lower box. A miraculous device of the devil, a motion-picture that talked, was just ending. At her feet the orchestra was assembling. The motion-picture faded out amid a scattered round of applause. Lights blazed and the orchestra burst into an ungodly rumpus.

She looked out over the seated multitude, scanning row upon row of illumined faces, black faces, white faces, yellow, tan, brown; bald heads, bobbed heads, kinky and straight heads; and upon every **countenance**,[15]

---

[15] **countenance**—face.

expectancy,—scowling expectancy in this case, smiling in that, **complacent**[16] here, amused there, commentative elsewhere, but everywhere suspense, **abeyance**,[17] anticipation.

Half a dozen people were ushered down the nearer aisle to reserved seats in the second row. Some of them caught sight of David and Ruth and waved to them. The chairs immediately behind them in the box were being shifted. "Hello, Tap!" Miss Cynthie saw David turn, rise, and shake hands with two men. One of them was large, bald and pink, emanating good cheer; the other short, thin, sallow with thick black hair and a sour **mien**.[18] Ruth also acknowledged their greeting. "This is my grandmother," David said proudly. "Miss Cynthie, meet my managers, Lou and Lee Goldman." "Pleased to meet you," managed Miss Cynthie. "Great lad, this boy of yours," said Lou Goldman. "Great little partner he's got, too," added Lee. They also settled back expectantly.

"Here we go!"

The curtain rose to reveal a cotton-field at dawn Pickers in blue denim overalls, bandanas, and wide-brimmed straws, or in gingham aprons and sunbonnets, were singing as they worked. Their voices, from clearest soprano to richest bass, blended in low **concordances**,[19] first simply humming a series of harmonies, until, gradually, came words, like figures forming in mist. As the sound grew, the mist cleared, the words came round and full, and the sun rose bringing light as if in answer to the song. The chorus swelled, the radiance grew, the two, as if **emanating**[20] from a single source, fused their crescendos, till at last they achieved a joint transcendence of tonal and visual brightness.

"Swell opener," said Lee Goldman.

---

[16] **complacent**—self-satisfied.

[17] **abeyance**—expectation.

[18] **mien**—bearing or manner.

[19] **concordances**—harmonies.

[20] **emanating**—originating; issuing.

"Ripe," agreed Lou.

David and Ruth arose. "Stay here and enjoy the show, Miss Cynthie. You'll see us again in a minute."

"Go to it, kids," said Lou Goldman.

"Yea—burn 'em up," said Lee.

Miss Cynthie hardly noted that she had been left, so absorbed was she in the spectacle. To her, the theatre had always been the **antithesis**[21] of the church. As the one was the refuge of righteousness, so the other was the stronghold of transgression. But this first scene awakened memories, captured and held her attention by offering a blend of truth and novelty. Having thus baited her interest, the show now proceeded to play it like the trout through swift-flowing waters of wickedness. Resist as it might, her mind was caught and drawn into the **impious**[22] subsequences.

The very music that had just rounded out so majestically now distorted itself into ragtime. The singers came forward and turned to dancers; boys, a crazy, swaying background, threw up their arms and kicked out their legs in a rhythmic jamboree; girls, an agile, brazen foreground, caught their skirts up to their hips and displayed their copper calves, knees, thighs, in shameless, incredible steps. Miss Cynthie turned dismayed eyes upon the audience, to discover that mob of sinners devouring it all with fond satisfaction. Then the dancers separated and with final abandon flung themselves off the stage in both directions.

Lee Goldman commented through the applause, "They work easy, them babies."

"Yea," said Lou. "Savin' the hot stuff for later."

Two black-faced cotton-pickers appropriated the scene, indulging in dialogue that their hearers found uproarious,

---

[21] **antithesis**—opposite.

[22] **impious**—not reverent; profane; disrespectful.

"Ah'm tired."

"Ah'm hongry."

"Dis job jes' wears me out."

"Starves me to death."

"Ah'm so tired—you know what Ah'd like to do?"

"What?"

"Ah'd like to go to sleep and dream I was sleepin'."

"What good dat do?"

"Den I could wake up and still be 'sleep."

"Well y' know what Ah'd like to do?"

"No. What?"

"Ah'd like to swaller me a hog and a hen."

"What good dat do?"

"Den Ah'd always be full o' ham and eggs."

"Ham? Shuh. Don't you know a hog has to be smoked 'fo' he's a ham?"

"Well, if I swaller him, he'll have a **smoke**[23] all around him, won' he?"

Presently Miss Cynthie was smiling like everyone else, but her smile soon fled. For the comics departed, and the dancing girls returned, this time in scant **travesties**[24] on their earlier voluminous costumes—tiny sunbonnets perched jauntily on one side of their glistening bobs, bandanas reduced to scarlet neck ribbons, **waists**[25] mere brassieres, skirts mere gingham sashes.

And now Miss Cynthie's whole body stiffened with a new and surpassing shock; her bright eyes first widened with unbelief, then slowly grew dull with misery. In the midst of a sudden great volley of applause her grandson had broken through that bevy of agile wantons[26] and begun to sing.

---

23 **smoke**—[slang] black person.

24 **travesties**—exaggerated imitations; caricatures.

25 **waists**—blouses; garments covering some or all of the area between the shoulders and the waist.

26 agile wantons—nimble, lewd persons.

He too was dressed as a cotton-picker, but a Beau Brummel[27] among cotton-pickers; his hat bore a pleated green band, his bandana was silk, his overalls blue satin, his shoes black patent leather. His eyes flashed, his teeth gleamed, his body swayed, his arms waved, his words came fast and clear. As he sang, his companions danced a concerted tap, uniformly wild, ecstatic. When he stopped singing, he himself began to dance, and without sacrificing crispness of execution, seemed to absorb into himself every measure of the energy which the girls, now merely standing off and swaying, had relinquished.

"Look at that boy go," said Lee Goldman.

"He ain't started yet," said Lou.

But surrounding comment, Dave's **virtuosity**,[28] the eager enthusiasm of the audience were all alike lost on Miss Cynthie. She sat with stricken eyes watching this boy whom she'd raised from a babe, taught right from wrong, brought up in the church, and endowed with her prayers, this child whom she had dreamed of seeing a preacher, a regular doctor, a tooth-doctor, a foot-doctor, at the very least an undertaker—sat watching him **disport**[29] himself for the benefit of a sinsick, flesh-hungry mob of lost souls, not one of whom knew or cared to know the loving kindness of God; sat watching a David she'd never foreseen, turned tool of the devil, disciple of lust, unholy prince among sinners.

For a long time she sat there watching with wretched eyes, saw portrayed on the stage David's arrival in Harlem, his escape from "old friends" who tried to dupe him; saw him working as a trap-drummer in a night-club, where he fell in love with Ruth, a dancer; not the gentle Ruth Miss Cynthie knew, but a wild and shameless

---

[27] Beau Brummel—(1778–1840), English aristocrat who established fashions in clothing; any fashionably dressed man.

[28] **virtuosity**—skill, fluency, and style demonstrated by a virtuoso, a masterful performer.

[29] **disport**—amuse or entertain.

young savage who danced like seven devils—in only a girdle and breastplates; saw the two of them join in a song-and-dance act that eventually made them Broadway headliners, an act presented *in toto*[30] as the pre-finale of this show. And not any of the melodies, not any of the sketches, not all the comic philosophy of the tired-and-hungry duo, gave her figure a moment's relaxation or brightened the dull defeat in her staring eyes. She sat apart, alone in the box, the symbol, the **epitome**[31] of supreme failure. Let the rest of the theatre be riotous, clamoring for more and more of Dave Tappen, "Tap," the greatest tapster of all time, idol of uptown and down-town New York. For her, they were **lauding**[32] simply an exhibition of sin which centered about her David.

"This'll run a year on Broadway," said Lee Goldman.

"Then we'll take it to Paris."

Encores and curtains with Ruth, and at last David came out on the stage alone. The clamor dwindled. And now he did something quite unfamiliar to even the most consistent of his followers. Softly, delicately, he began to tap a routine designed to fit a particular song. When he had established the rhythm, he began to sing the song:

> *"Oh I danced with the gal with the hole in her stockin',*
> *And her toe kep' a-kickin' and her heel kep' a-knockin'*
>
> *Come up, Jesse, and get a drink o' gin,*
> *'Cause you near to the heaven as you'll ever get ag'in—"*

As he danced and sang this song, frequently smiling across at Miss Cynthie, a visible change transformed her. She leaned forward incredulously, listened intently, then settled back in limp wonder. Her bewildered eyes

---

[30] *In toto*—completely.

[31] **epitome**—embodiment.

[32] **lauding**—praising.

turned on the crowd, on those **serried**[33] rows of **shriftless**[34] sinners. And she found in their faces now an overwhelmingly curious thing: a grin, a universal grin, a gleeful and sinless grin such as not the nakedest chorus in the performance had produced. In a few seconds, with her own song, David had dwarfed into unimportance, wiped off their faces, swept out of their minds every trace of what had seemed to be sin; had reduced it all to mere trivial detail and revealed these revelers as a crowd of children, enjoying the **guileless**[35] antics of another child. And Miss Cynthie whispered her discovery aloud:

"Bless my soul! They didn't mean nothin' . . . They jes' didn't see no harm in it—"

"Then I danced with the gal with the dimple in her cheek,
And if she'd 'a' kep' a-smilin' I'd 'a' danced for a week—

Come up, Jesse—"

The crowd laughed, clapped their hands, whistled. Someone threw David a bright yellow flower. "From Broadway!"

He caught the flower. A hush fell. He said:

"I'm really happy tonight, folks. Y'see this flower? Means success, don't it? Well, listen. The one who is really responsible for my success is here tonight with me. Now what do you think o' that?"

The hush deepened.

"Y'know folks, I'm sump'm like Adam—I never had no mother. But I've got a grandmother. Down home everybody calls her Miss Cynthie. And everybody loves her. Take that song I just did for you. Miss Cynthie taught me that when I wasn't knee-high to a cricket. But that wasn't all she taught me. Far back as I

---

[33] **serried**—pressed together.
[34] **shriftless**—unconfessed and, thus, unrepentant.
[35] **guileless**—innocent; naive.

can remember, she used to always say one thing: 'Son, do like a church steeple—aim high and go straight.' And for doin' it—" he grinned, contemplating the flower—"I get this."

He strode across to the edge of the stage that touched Miss Cynthie's box. He held up the flower.

"So y'see, folks, this isn't mine. It's really Miss Cynthie's." He leaned over to hand it to her. Miss Cynthie's last trace of doubt was swept away. She drew a deep breath of revelation; her bewilderment vanished, her **redoubtable**[36] composure returned, her eyes lighted up; and no one but David, still holding the flower toward her, heard her sharply whispered reprimand:

"Keep it, you fool you. Where's yo' manners—givin' 'way what somebody give you?"

David grinned:

"Take it, **tyro**.[37] What you tryin' to do—crab[38] my act?"

Thereupon, Miss Cynthie, smiling at him with bright, meaningful eyes, leaned over without rising from her chair, jerked a tiny twig off the stem of the flower, then sat decisively back, resolutely folding her arms, with only a leaf in her hand.

"This'll do me," she said.

The finale didn't matter. People filed out of the theatre. Miss Cynthie sat awaiting her children, her foot absently patting time to the orchestra's jazz recessional. Perhaps she was thinking, "God moves in a mysterious way," but her lips were unquestionably forming the words:

"—danced with the gal—hole in her stockin'—
—toe kep' a-kickin'—heel kep' a-knockin'—"

---

[36] **redoubtable**—awesome; formidable.

[37] **tyro**—beginner.

[38] **crab**—interfere with; spoil.

QUESTIONS TO CONSIDER

1. Which of the wonders that Miss Cynthie encounters in New York City particularly delight or impress her?

2. What contrasts does Fisher emphasize in "Miss Cynthie"?

3. Why do you think David insists on showing Miss Cynthie what he does instead of simply telling her?

4. How do you explain Miss Cynthie's sudden change of attitude toward David's audience at the end of the story?

5. How does Fisher's story serve as a way of celebrating Harlem?

City Style

Three Harlem flappers are shown strolling down Seventh Avenue, one of the community's main streets.

▲
Harlem Renaissance artist Aaron Douglas's interpretation of the
biblical figure of the Prodigal Son sets the story of his downfall in
a 1920s cabaret.

▲

Harlem High Life Wearing raccoon coats and with a Cadillac, the young couple in this image by photographer James Van Der Zee displays the glamour and sophistication that Harlemites aspired to in the 1920s.

Painted in 1934, Archibald Motley, Jr.'s *Black Belt* depicts the vibrant street life that marked African-American communities such as Harlem.

▼

▲

This photo of a Harlem street scene by Van Der Zee shows two important elements in the community's life: churches and nightclubs.

Struggling with
Injustice

Returning Soldiers

BY W.E.B. DUBOIS

Historian, sociologist, and leading spokesperson for early twentieth-century civil rights, Dr. W.E.B. DuBois (1868–1963) helped create the National Association for the Advancement of Colored People (NAACP). From 1910 to 1934, he served as editor of its publication The Crisis, *the most influential and highly read African-American publication of its time. DuBois believed in public protest against the legal and personal injustices suffered by many African Americans. He also believed in encouraging "the talented tenth" of his race to excel by becoming doctors, lawyers, teachers, and, especially, artists. In the following editorial, DuBois urges black World War I veterans— who had fought against tyranny on European battlefields—to fight "the forces of hell" at home.*

We are returning from war! *The Crisis* and tens of thousands of black men were drafted into a great struggle. For bleeding France and what she means and has meant and will mean to us and humanity and against the threat of German race arrogance, we fought gladly and to the last drop of blood; for America and her highest ideals, we fought in far-off hope; for the dominant southern

oligarchy[1] entrenched in Washington, we fought in bitter **resignation.**[2] For the America that represents and gloats in lynching, **disfranchisement,**[3] caste, brutality and devilish insult—for this, in the hateful upturning and mixing of things, we were forced by **vindictive**[4] fate to fight, also.

But today we return! We return from the slavery of uniform which the world's madness demanded us to **don**[5] to the freedom of civil garb.[6] We stand again to look America squarely in the face and call a spade a spade. We sing: This country of ours, despite all its better souls have done and dreamed, is yet a shameful land.

It *lynches.*

And lynching is barbarism of a degree of contemptible nastiness unparalleled in human history. Yet for fifty years we have lynched two Negroes a week, and we have kept this up right through the war.

It *disfranchises* its own citizens.

Disfranchisement is the deliberate theft and robbery of the only protection of poor against rich and black against white. The land that disfranchises its citizens and calls itself a democracy lies and knows it lies.

It encourages *ignorance.*

It has never really tried to educate the Negro. A dominant minority does not want Negroes educated. It wants servants, dogs, whores and monkeys. And when this land allows a **reactionary**[7] group by its stolen political power to force as many black folk into these categories as it possibly can, it cries in contemptible

---

[1] **oligarchy**—form of government in which a select group controls the power.

[2] **resignation**—unresistant acceptance; submission.

[3] **disfranchisement**—depriving people of their rights.

[4] **vindictive**—revengeful.

[5] **don**—put on; wear.

[6] civil garb—civilian clothes.

[7] **reactionary**—opposed to progress; extremely conservative.

hypocrisy: "They threaten us with **degeneracy**;[8] they cannot be educated."

It *steals* from us.

It organizes industry to cheat us. It cheats us out of our land; it cheats us out of our labor. It confiscates our savings. It reduces our wages. It raises our rent. It steals our profit. It taxes us without representation. It keeps us consistently and universally poor, and then feeds us on charity and **derides**[9] our poverty.

It *insults* us.

It has organized a nation-wide and latterly a world-wide propaganda of deliberate and continuous insult and defamation of black blood wherever found. It decrees that it shall not be possible in travel nor residence, work nor play, education nor instruction for a black man to exist without **tacit**[10] or open acknowledgment of his inferiority to the dirtiest white dog. And it looks upon any attempt to question or even discuss this **dogma**[11] as arrogance, unwarranted assumption and treason.

This is the country to which we Soldiers of Democracy return. This is the fatherland for which we fought! But it is *our* fatherland. It was right for us to fight. The faults of *our* country are *our* faults. Under similar circumstances, we would fight again. But by the God of Heaven, we are cowards and fools if now that that war is over, we do not marshal every ounce of our brain and brawn to fight a sterner, longer, more unbending battle against the forces of hell in our own land.

We *return*.

We *return from fighting*.

We *return fighting*.

---

[8] **degeneracy**—inferiority.

[9] **derides**—ridicules; mocks; scoffs at.

[10] **tacit**—understood; implied rather than stated.

[11] **dogma**—belief.

Make way for Democracy! We saved it in France, and by the Great Jehovah, we will save it in the United States of America, or know the reason why.

QUESTIONS TO CONSIDER

1. What is the thesis of this editorial?

2. How would you characterize the writer?

3. What response does the writer seem to want from his readers?

4. What is the structure of this editorial? How does the structure serve to emphasize the author's views?

If We Must Die

BY CLAUDE McKAY

*During the bloody summer of 1919, a year after World War I
ended, more than twenty-five race riots broke out in the United
States. The two most violent occurred in Omaha and in Chicago.
Chicago's riot lasted thirteen days, and by its end 38 people were
dead (23 blacks, 15 whites), 537 were injured, and 1,000 black
families were homeless. One historian suggests that these riots
were the result of "large-scale Negro migration to the North, indus-
trial labor competition, overcrowding in urban ghettos, and greater
militancy among black war veterans who had fought 'to preserve
democracy.'" Poet Claude McKay (1889–1948) responded to the
riots with the following poem, a sonnet considered so radical and
inflammatory that one black editor refused to publish it, and Alain
Locke, the influential Harlem Renaissance editor, omitted it from
his definitive anthology* The New Negro. *"If We Must Die,"
written in 1919, foreshadows the insistence of many Harlem
Renaissance writers on defining a proud African-American identity.*

If we must die, let it not be like hogs
Hunted and penned in an **inglorious**[1] spot,
While round us bark the mad and hungry dogs,
Making their mock at our **accursed**[2] lot.
If we must die, O let us nobly die,
So that our precious blood may not be shed
In vain; then even the monsters we defy
Shall be constrained to honor us though dead!
O kinsmen! we must meet the common foe!
Though far outnumbered let us show us brave,
And for their thousand blows deal one deathblow!
What though before us lies the open grave?
Like men we'll face the murderous, cowardly pack,
Pressed to the wall, dying, but fighting back!

---

[1] **inglorious**—disgraceful.

[2] **accursed**—doomed.

QUESTIONS TO CONSIDER

1. In what three animal images does the speaker portray the oppressors?

2. Why does the speaker not specify why "we must die"?

3. Why does the speaker argue for a noble death?

4. Why do you think black editors found this poem too radical to publish?

Strong Men

BY STERLING A. BROWN

Unlike other Harlem Renaissance writers, Sterling A. Brown (1901–1989) spent little time in New York. The son of a prominent Washington, D.C., professor, he graduated from Williams College in 1922 and received his master's degree from Harvard. After three years of teaching in Virginia, he joined the Howard University faculty in Washington, D.C., and taught there until he retired in 1969. Along with Langston Hughes and others, Brown challenged the belief that the use of black dialect was unsuitable for serious poetry. In "Strong Men," a poem whose form and title is indebted to the poetry of Carl Sandburg (1878–1967), Brown employs both dialect and standard English to summarize white injustices and the indomitable spirit and strength of blacks.

The strong men keep coming on.

Sandburg

They dragged you from homeland,
They chained you in **coffles**,[1]
They huddled you spoon-fashion in filthy hatches,
They sold you to give a few gentlemen ease.

They broke you in like oxen,
They **scourged**[2] you,
They branded you,
They made your women breeders,
They swelled your numbers with bastards. . . .
They taught you the religion they disgraced.

You sang:
    Keep a-inchin' along
    Lak a po' inch worm. . . .

You sang:
    Bye and bye
    I'm gonna lay down dis heaby load. . . .

You sang:
Walk togedder, chillen,
Dontcha git weary. . . .
        The strong men keep a-comin' on
        The strong men git stronger.

They point with pride to the roads you built for them,
They ride in comfort over the rails you laid for them.
They put hammers in your hands
And said—Drive so much before sundown.

---

[1] **coffles**—groups or files of slaves chained together.
[2] **scourged**—whipped; beat.

You sang:
   Ain't no hammah
   In dis lan',
   Strikes lak mine, bebby,
   Strikes lak mine.

They cooped you in their kitchens,
They penned you in their factories,
They gave you the jobs that they were too good for,
They tried to guarantee happiness to themselves
By **shunting**[3] dirt and misery to you.

You sang:
   Me an' muh baby gonna shine, shine
   Me an' muh baby gonna shine.
         The strong men keep a-comin' on
         The strong men git stronger. . . .

They bought off some of your leaders
You stumbled, as blind men will . . .
They coaxed you, unwontedly[4] soft-voiced. . . .
You followed a way.
Then laughed as usual.

They heard the laugh and wondered;
Uncomfortable;
Unadmitting a deeper terror. . . .
         The strong men keep a-comin' on
         Gittin' stronger. . . .

---

[3] **shunting**—handing over; assigning.
[4] unwontedly—unusually.

What, from the slums
Where they have hemmed you,
What, from the tiny huts
They could not keep from you—
What reaches them
Making them ill at ease, fearful?
Today they shout prohibition at you
"Thou shalt not this"
"Thou shalt not that"
"Reserved for whites only"
You laugh.

One thing they cannot prohibit—
> *The strong men . . . coming on*
> *The strong men gittin' stronger.*
> *Strong men. . . .*
> *Stronger. . . .*

QUESTIONS TO CONSIDER

1. What injustices does Brown list in his poem?

2. What is the connection between the content of the poem and the two levels of language—standard English and black dialect—used in the poem?

3. What is the connection between the content of the poem and the use of italicized and non-italicized lines?

4. Why do you think Brown incorporates snatches of songs and spirituals?

Yet Do I Marvel

BY COUNTEE CULLEN

*Before he was twenty, New York University student Countee Cullen
(1903–1946) won a national poetry contest open to undergraduates
in all American universities. Soon after graduation in 1925, Cullen
became a published poet and a graduate student at Harvard
University. Like several of the early Harlem Renaissance poets,
Cullen never abandoned rhyme scheme or such traditional forms as
the sonnet, nor did he use dialect or the rhythms of jazz. With elegant language and classical references, Cullen wrote powerful
poems about past and present injustices. In "Yet Do I Marvel,"
Cullen comments on injustice.*

> I doubt not[1] God is good, well-meaning, kind,
> And did He[2] stoop to **quibble**[3] could tell why
> The little buried mole continues blind,
> Why flesh that mirrors Him must some day die,

---

[1] I doubt not—"I don't doubt that."
[2] did He—if He would.
[3] **quibble**—argue about insignificant distinctions.

Make plain the reason tortured Tantalus[4]
Is baited by the fickle fruit, declare
If merely brute **caprice**[5] dooms Sisyphus[6]
To struggle up a never-ending stair.
Inscrutable[7] His ways are, and immune
To **catechism**[8] by a mind too strewn
With petty cares to slightly understand
What awful brain compels His awful hand.
Yet do I marvel at this curious thing:
To make a poet black, and bid him sing!

---

[4] Tantalus—in Greek mythology, a king whose punishment in the underworld was to stand in water that receded when he tried to drink and under a fruit tree that receded when he reached for fruit to eat.

[5] **caprice**—whim; impulse.

[6] Sisyphus—in Greek mythology, a king condemned to roll a stone up a mountain only to have it roll down again.

[7] **Inscrutable**—unknowable; incomprehensible.

[8] **catechism**—question-and-answer mode of learning.

QUESTIONS TO CONSIDER

1. What kinds of things does Cullen want God to explain?

2. Why would the poet use the word *quibble?* What do you think he believes about the importance of blindness and death?

3. What do the ancient kings Tantalus and Sisyphus have in common with a black poet?

4. What does the word *awful* mean? Why do you think the poet chose to repeat it?

5. Why does Cullen "marvel"?

A Black Man Talks of Reaping

BY ARNA BONTEMPS

Born in Louisiana, Arna Bontemps (1902–1973) grew up in California and was educated at various Seventh Day Adventist religious schools. After briefly working in the Los Angeles post office, Bontemps moved to New York in 1924 and taught at Harlem's Seventh Day Adventist Academy. By 1928, his poems were being published and were winning prizes. Eventually, Bontemps became a librarian and began a collection that made Fisk University an important center for the study of African-American heritage. In "A Black Man Talks of Reaping," Bontemps reviews the life of a black man and what being black has cost him and his children.

I have sown beside all waters in my day.
I planted deep within my heart the fear
That wind or fowl would take the grain away.
I planted safe against this stark, lean year.

I scattered seed enough to plant the land
In rows from Canada to Mexico.
But for my reaping only what the hand
Can hold at once is all that I can show.

Yet what I sowed and what the orchard yields
My brother's sons are gathering stalk and root,
Small wonder then my children **glean**[1] in fields
They have not sown, and feed on bitter fruit.

---

[1] **glean**—gather grain left after reaping is done.

QUESTIONS TO CONSIDER

1. What are the differences among sowing, reaping, and gleaning? At which of these three activities has the speaker been most successful?

2. Who do you think the speaker means by his "brother's sons"?

3. How do you explain why it is "small wonder" that the speaker's children "glean in fields"?

4. What words would you use to characterize the tone of this poem?

Sanctuary

BY NELLA LARSEN

When Nella Larsen (1893–1964) published her novel Quicksand *in 1928, critics were quick to praise the rich complexity of the work. Like the author, the protagonist of the novel was the child of a black West Indian father and a Danish mother. Larsen trained as a nurse, completing her course in 1915. For the next six years, she worked in various hospitals and for the New York Department of Health before taking a job at the Countee Cullen branch of the New York City library system. In addition to* Quicksand, *Larsen wrote a second novel,* Passing, *and some short stories. In 1931, she was publicly accused of plagiarizing the idea for the following short story, "Sanctuary" (1930). Although Larsen defended herself, she never recovered and wrote little afterwards. Whether or not the idea is original, Larsen's story is a wonderful presentation of a woman who faces a difficult choice between two injustices.*

I

On the Southern coast, between Merton and Shawboro,[1] there is a strip of desolation some half a mile

---

[1] Merton and Shawboro—towns in North Carolina.

wide and nearly ten miles long between the sea and old fields of ruined plantations. Skirting the edge of this narrow jungle is a partly grown-over road which still shows traces of furrows made by the wheels of wagons that have long since rotted away or been cut into fire-wood. This road is little used, now that the state has built its new highway a bit to the west and wagons are less numerous than automobiles.

In the forsaken road a man was walking swiftly. But in spite of his hurry, at every step he set down his feet with infinite care, for the night was windless and the heavy silence intensified each sound; even the breaking of a twig could be plainly heard and the man had need of caution as well as haste.

Before a lonely cottage that shrank timidly back from the road the man hesitated a moment, then struck out across the patch of green in front of it. Stepping behind a clump of bushes close to the house, he looked in through the lighted window at Annie Poole, standing at her kitchen table mixing the supper biscuits.

He was a big, black man with pale brown eyes in which there was an odd mixture of fear and amazement. The light showed streaks of gray soil on his heavy, sweating face and great hands, and on his torn clothes. In his woolly hair clung bits of dried leaves and dead grass.

He made a gesture as if to tap on the window, but turned away to the door instead. Without knocking he opened it and went in.

2

The woman's brown gaze was immediately on him, though she did not move. She said, "You ain't in no hurry, is you, Jim Hammer?" It wasn't, however, entirely a question.

"Ah's in trubble, Mis' Poole," the man explained, his voice shaking, his fingers twitching.

"W'at you done now?"

"Shot a man, Mis' Poole."

"Trufe?" The woman seemed calm. But the word was spat out.

"Yas'm. Shot 'im." In the man's tone was something of wonder, as if he himself could not quite believe that he had really done this thing which he affirmed.

"Daid?"

"Dunno, Mis' Poole. Dunno."

"White man o' black?"

"Cain't say, Mis' Poole. White man, Ah reckons."

Annie Poole looked at him with cold contempt. She was a tiny, withered woman—fifty perhaps—with a wrinkled face the color of old copper, framed by a crinkly mass of white hair.

But about her small figure was some quality of hardness that **belied**[2] her appearance of frailty. At last she spoke, boring her sharp little eyes into those of the anxious creature before her.

"An' w'at am you lookin' foh me to do 'bout et?"

"Jes' lemme stop till dey's gone by. Hide me till dey passes. Reckon dey ain't fur off now." His begging voice changed to a frightened whimper. "Foh de Lawd's sake, Mis' Poole, lemme stop."

And why, the woman inquired **caustically**,[3] should she run the dangerous risk of hiding him?

"Obadiah, he'd lemme stop ef he was to home," the man whined.

Annie Poole sighed. "Yas," she admitted slowly, reluctantly, "Ah spec' he would. Obadiah, he's too good to you all no 'count trash." Her slight shoulders lifted in a hopeless shrug.

"Yas, Ah reckon he'd do et. Emspecial' seein' how he allus set such a heap o' store by you. Cain't see w'at foh, mahse'f. Ah shuah don' see nuffin' in you but a heap o' dirt."

---

[2] **belied**—contradicted.

[3] **caustically**—sarcastically.

But a look of irony, of cunning, of **complicity**[4] passed over her face. She went on, "Still, 'siderin' all an' all, how Obadiah's right fon' o' you, an' how white folks is white folks, Ah'm a-gwine hide you dis one time."

Crossing the kitchen, she opened a door leading into a small bedroom, saying, "Git yo'se'f in dat dere feather baid an' Ah'm a-gwine put de clo's on de top. Don' reckon dey'll fin' you ef dey does look foh you in mah house. An Ah don' spec' dey'll go foh to do dat. Not lessen you been keerless an' let 'em smell you out gittin' hyah." She turned on him a withering look. "But you allus been triflin'. Cain't do nuffin' propah. An' Ah'm a-tellin' you ef dey warn's white folks an' you a po' black, Ah shuah wouldn't be lettin' you mess up mah feather baid dis ebenin', 'cose Ah jes' plain don' went you hyah. Ah done kep' mahse'f outen trubble all mah life. So's Obadiah."

"Ah's powahful 'bliged to you, Mis' Poole. You shuah am one good 'omen. De Lawd'll mos' suttinly—"

Annie Poole cut him off. "Dis ain't no time foh all dat kin' o' **fiddle-de-roll**.[5] Ah does mah duty as Ah sees et 'shout no thanks from you. Ef de Lawd had gib you a white face 'stead o' dat dere black one, Ah shuah would turn you out. Now hush yo' mouf an' git yo'se'f in. An' don' git movin' and scrunchin' undah dose covahs and git yo'se'f kotched in mah house."

Without further comment the man did as he was told. After he had laid his soiled body and grimy garments between her snowy sheets, Annie Poole carefully rearranged the covering and placed piles of freshly laundered linen on top. Then she gave a pat here and there, eyed the result, and, finding it satisfactory, went back to her cooking.

---

[4] **complicity**—sharing in wrongdoing.
[5] **fiddle-de-roll**—foolish talk, from *folderol*.

3

Jim Hammer settled down to the **racking**⁶ business of waiting until the approaching danger should have passed him by. Soon savory odors seeped in to him and he realized that he was hungry. He wished that Annie Poole would bring him something to eat. Just one biscuit. But she wouldn't, he knew. Not she. She was a hard one, Obadiah's mother.

By and by he fell into a sleep from which he was dragged back by the rumbling sounds of wheels in the road outside. For a second fear clutched so tightly at him that he almost leaped from the suffocating shelter of the bed in order to make some active attempt to escape the horror that his capture meant. There was a spasm at his heart, a pain so sharp, so slashing, that he had to suppress an impulse to cry out. He felt himself falling. Down, down, down . . . Everything grew dim and very distant in his memory . . . Vanished . . . Came rushing back.

Outside there was silence. He strained his ears. Nothing. No footsteps. No voices. They had gone on then. Gone without even stopping to ask Annie Poole if she had seen him pass that way. A sigh of relief slipped from him. His thick lips curled in an ugly, cunning smile. It had been smart of him to think of coming to Obadiah's mother's to hide. She was an old demon, but he was safe in her house.

He lay a short while longer, listening intently, and, hearing nothing, started to get up. But immediately he stopped, his yellow eyes glowing like pale flames. He had heard the unmistakable sound of men coming toward the house. Swiftly he slid back into the heavy, hot stuffiness of the bed and lay listening fearfully.

The terrifying sounds drew nearer. Slowly. Heavily. Just for a moment he thought they were not coming in—

---

⁶ **racking**—torturous.

they took so long. But there was a light knock and the noise of a door being opened. His whole body went **taut**.[7] His feet felt frozen, his hands clammy, his tongue like a weighted, dying thing. His pounding heart made it hard for his straining ears to hear what they were saying out there.

"Evenin', Mistah Lowndes." Annie Poole's voice sounded as it always did, sharp and dry.

There was no answer. Or had he missed it? With slow care he shifted his position, bringing his head nearer the edge of the bed. Still he heard nothing. What were they waiting for? Why didn't they ask about him?

Annie Poole, it seemed, was of the same mind. "Ah don' reckon youall done **traipsed**[8] way out hyah jes' foh yo' healf," she hinted.

"There's bad news for you, Annie, I'm 'fraid." The sheriff's voice was low and queer. Jim Hammer visualized him standing out there—a tall, stooped man, his white tobacco stained mustache drooping limply at the ends, his nose hooked and sharp, his eyes blue and cold. Bill Lowndes was a hard one too. And white.

"W'atall bad news, Mistah Lowndes?" The woman put the question quietly, directly.

"Obadiah " the sheriff began hesitated began again. "Obadiah—ah—er—he's outside, Annie. I'm 'fraid—"

"Shucks! You done missed. Obadiah, he ain't done nuffin', Mistah Lowndes. Obadiah!" she called **stridently**,[9] "Obadiah! git hyah an' splain yo'se'f."

But Obadiah didn't answer, didn't come in. Other men came in. Came in with steps that dragged and halted. No one spoke. Not even Annie Poole. Something was laid carefully upon the floor.

---

[7] **taut**—tight; tense.

[8] **traipsed**—wandered.

[9] **stridently**—loudly and harshly.

"Obadiah, chile," his mother said softly, "Obadiah, chile." Then, with sudden alarm, "He ain't daid, is he? Mistah Lowndes! Obadiah, he ain't daid?"

Jim Hammer didn't catch the answer to that pleading question. A new fear was stealing over him.

"There was a to-do, Annie," Bill Lowndes explained gently, "at the garage back o' the factory. Fellow tryin' to steal tires. Obadiah heerd a noise an' run out with two or three others. Scared the rascal all right. Fired off his gun an' run. We allow et to be Jim Hammer. Picked up his cap back there. Never was no 'count. Thievin' an' sly. But we'll git 'im, Annie. We'll git 'im."

The man huddled in the feather bed prayed silently. "Oh, Lawd! Ah didn't go to do et. Not Obadiah, Lawd. You knows dat. You knows et." And into his frenzied brain came the thought that it would be better for him to get up and go out to them before Annie Poole gave him away. For he was lost now. With all his great strength he tried to get himself out of the bed. But he couldn't.

"Oh, Lawd!" he moaned. "Oh, Lawd!" His thoughts were bitter and they ran through his mind like panic. He knew that it had come to pass as it said somewhere in the Bible about the wicked. The Lord had stretched out his hand and **smitten**[10] him. He was paralyzed. He couldn't move hand or foot. He moaned again. It was all there was left for him to do. For in the terror of this new **calamity**[11] that had come upon him he had forgotten the waiting danger which was so near out there in the kitchen.

His hunters, however, didn't hear him. Bill Lowndes was saying, "We been a-lookin' for Jim out along the old road. Figured he'd make tracks for Shawboro. You ain't noticed anybody pass this evenin', Annie?"

The reply came promptly, unwaveringly. "No, Ah ain't sees nobody pass. Not yet."

---

[10] **smitten**—struck; archaic past tense form of *smite*.

[11] **calamity**—great misfortune.

4

Jim Hammer caught his breath.

"Well," the sheriff concluded, "we'll be gittin' along. Obadiah was a mighty fine boy. Ef they was all like him—I'm sorry, Annie. Anything I c'n do, let me know."

"Thank you, Mistah Lowndes."

With the sound of the door closing on the departing men, power to move came back to the man in the bedroom. He pushed his dirt-caked feet out from the covers and rose up, but crouched down again. He wasn't cold now, but hot all over and burning. Almost he wished that Bill Lowndes and his men had taken him with them.

Annie Poole had come into the room.

It seemed a long time before Obadiah's mother spoke. When she did there were no tears, no reproaches; but there was a raging fury in her voice as she lashed out, "Git outer mah feather baid, Jim Hammer, an' outen mah house, an' don' nevah stop thankin' yo' Jesus he done gib you dat black face."

QUESTIONS TO CONSIDER

1. What details directly or indirectly suggest the time and place of the story?

2. What is Annie Poole's opinion of Jim Hammer?

3. How might the moral and upright Annie Poole justify her comment that she hadn't seen anyone pass that way?

4. What does Larsen's story suggest about the African-American struggle for justice?

Asserting Freedom

▲
Celebrating Heritage Meta Warrick Fuller evoked African oral tradition in her 1937 sculpture *Talking Skull*.

▲
Sculptor Meta Warrick Fuller's 1919 sculpture
Mary Turner (A Silent Protest Against Mob Violence)
memorializes a victim of lynching.

Fear and Hope Harlem Renaissance artist Sargent Johnson's 1933 sculpture *Forever Free* celebrates the struggles of African Americans for liberty and justice.

Painted in 1930, Aaron Douglas's *Rise, Shine, for Thy Light Has Come!* expresses a joyous anticipation of freedom. ▶

▲

Loïs Mailou Jones (1905–1998) taught design, drawing, and watercolor at Howard University from 1930 to 1977. Her own painting was influenced by the painters she met in her studies in France and by African motifs she investigated in a design class at Columbia University in New York. *Les Fétiches* [the fetishes or religious spirits] was painted in Paris in 1938. In it, Jones presents masks from five African groups.

Lois Mailou Jones, *The Ascent of Ethiopia,* 1932, Oil on Canvas, 23 1/2 x 17 1/4 in., Milwaukee Art Museum, Purchase, African-American Acquisition Fund, matching funds from Suzanne and Richard Piopor, with additional support from Arthur and Dorothy Nelle Sanders, Photo credit: Larry Sanders

▲

Jones's 1932 painting *The Ascent of Ethiopia* links ancient Africa and the modern world.

Being an
Individual

Criteria of Negro Art

BY W.E.B. DUBOIS

As a founder and important spokesperson for the National Association for the Advancement of Colored People (NAACP), W. E. B. DuBois (1868–1963) not only edited The Crisis, the NAACP's official magazine, but he regularly addressed the NAACP's gatherings. In 1926, DuBois spoke at an NAACP meeting in Chicago on the subject of art's significance in the fight for civil rights. DuBois had come to believe that through artistic achievement, African Americans would assert their racial and personal pride and at last be recognized as full and equal citizens. In "Criteria of Negro Art," DuBois passionately argues that art and propaganda are one.

I do not doubt but there are some in this audience who are a little disturbed at the subject of this meeting, and particularly at the subject I have chosen. Such people are thinking something like this: "How is it that an organization like this, a group of radicals trying to bring new things into the world, a fighting organization which has come up out of the blood and dust of battle, struggling for the right of black men to be ordinary human beings—how is it that an organization of this kind can turn aside to talk about Art? After all, what have we who are slaves and black to do with Art?"

Or perhaps there are others who feel a certain relief and are saying, "After all it is rather satisfactory after all this talk about rights and fighting to sit and dream of something which leaves a nice taste in the mouth."

Let me tell you that neither of these groups is right. The thing we are talking about tonight is part of the great fight we are carrying on and it represents a forward and an upward look—a pushing onward. You and I have been **breasting**[1] hills; we have been climbing upward; there has been progress and we can see it day by day looking back along blood-filled paths. But as you go through the valleys and over the foothills, so long as you are climbing, the direction,—north, south, east or west,—is of less importance. But when gradually the **vista**[2] widens and you begin to see the world at your feet and the far horizon, then it is time to know more precisely **whither**[3] you are going and what you really want.

What do we want? What is the thing we are after? As it was phrased last night it had a certain truth: We want to be Americans, full-fledged Americans, with all the rights of other American citizens. But is that all? Do we want simply to be Americans? Once in a while through all of us there flashes some **clairvoyance**,[4] some clear idea, of what America really is. We who are dark can see America in a way that white Americans can not. And seeing our country thus, are we satisfied with its present goals and ideals?

---

[1] **breasting**—climbing.

[2] **vista**—view.

[3] **whither**—where.

[4] **clairvoyance**—view of things beyond the range of the sense organs; intuition.

In the high school where I studied we learned most of Scott's "Lady of the Lake"[5] by heart. In after life once it was my privilege to see the lake. It was Sunday. It was quiet. You could glimpse the deer wandering in unbroken forests; you could hear the soft ripple of romance on the waters. Around me fell the cadence of that poetry of my youth. I fell asleep full of the enchantment of the Scottish border. A new day broke and with it came a sudden rush of **excursionists**.[6] They were mostly Americans and they were loud and strident. They poured upon the little pleasure boat,—men with their hats a little on one side and drooping cigars in the wet corners of their mouths; women who shared their conversation with the world. They all tried to get everywhere first. They pushed other people out of the way. They made all sorts of incoherent noises and gestures so that the quiet home folk and the visitors from other lands silently and half-wonderingly gave way before them. They struck a note not evil but wrong. They carried, perhaps, a sense of strength and accomplishment, but their hearts had no conception of the beauty which pervaded this holy place.

If you tonight suddenly should become full-fledged Americans; if your color faded, or the color line here in Chicago was miraculously forgotten; suppose, too, you became at the same time rich and powerful;—what is it that you would want? What would you immediately seek? Would you buy the most powerful of motor cars and outrace Cook County? Would you buy the most elaborate estate on the North Shore? Would you be a Rotarian or a Lion or a What-not of the very last degree? Would you wear the most striking clothes, give the richest dinners and buy the longest press notices?

Even as you visualize such ideals you know in your hearts that these are not the things you really want. You realize this sooner than the average white American

---

[5] Scott's "Lady of the Lake"—poem by Sir Walter Scott (1771–1832).
[6] **excursionists**—adventurers; travelers.

because, pushed aside as we have been in America, there has come to us not only a certain distaste for the **tawdry**[7] and **flamboyant**[8] but a vision of what the world could be if it were really a beautiful world; if we had the true spirit; if we had the Seeing Eye, the Cunning Hand, the Feeling Heart; if we had, to be sure, not perfect happiness, but plenty of good hard work, the inevitable suffering that always comes with life; sacrifice and waiting, all that— but, nevertheless, lived in a world where men know, where men create, where they realize themselves and where they enjoy life. It is that sort of a world we want to create for ourselves and for all America.

After all, who shall describe Beauty? What is it? I remember tonight four beautiful things: The Cathedral at Cologne,[9] a forest in stone, set in light and changing shadow, echoing with sunlight and solemn song; a village of the Veys[10] in West Africa, a little thing of mauve and purple, quiet, lying and shining in the sun; a black and velvet room where on a throne rests, in old and yellowing marble, the broken curves of the Venus of Milo;[11] a single phrase of music in the Southern South—utter melody, haunting and appealing, suddenly arising out of night and eternity, beneath the moon.

Such is Beauty. Its variety is infinite, its possibility is endless. In normal life all may have it and have it yet again. The world is full of it; and yet today the mass of human beings are choked away from it, and their lives distorted and made ugly. This is not only wrong, it is silly. Who shall right this well-nigh[12] universal failing? Who shall let this world be beautiful? Who shall restore to men the glory of sunsets and the peace of quiet sleep?

---

[7] **tawdry**—showy; cheap-looking.

[8] **flamboyant**—ornate, often excessively so.

[9] Cathedral at Cologne —medieval cathedral in Germany.

[10] Veys—one of the Mandingo peoples of Senegal.

[11] Venus of Milo—ancient statue in the Louvre Museum, Paris; found on the Greek island of Melos.

[12] well-nigh—very nearly; almost.

We black folk may help for we have within us as a race new stirrings; stirrings of the beginning of a new appreciation of joy, of a new desire to create, of a new will to be; as though in this morning of group life we had awakened from some sleep that at once dimly mourns the past and dreams a splendid future; and there has come the conviction that the Youth that is here today, the Negro Youth, is a different kind of Youth, because in some new way it bears this mighty prophecy on its breast, with a new realization of itself, with new determination for all mankind.

What has this Beauty to do with the world? What has Beauty to do with Truth and Goodness—with the facts of the world and the right actions of men? "Nothing," the artists rush to answer. They may be right. I am but an humble disciple of art and cannot presume to say. I am one who tells the truth and exposes evil and seeks with Beauty and for Beauty to set the world right. That somehow, somewhere eternal and perfect Beauty sits above Truth and Right I can conceive, but here and now and in the world in which I work they are for me unseparated and inseparable. . . .

The question comes next as to the interpretation of these new stirrings, of this new spirit: Of what is the colored artist capable? We have had on the part of both colored and white people singular **unanimity**[13] of judgment in the past. Colored people have said: "This work must be inferior because it comes from colored people." White people have said: "It is inferior because it is done by colored people." But today there is coming to both the realization that the work of the black man is not always inferior. Interesting stories come to us. A professor in the University of Chicago read to a class that had studied literature a passage of poetry and asked them to guess the author. They guessed a goodly company from

---

13 **unanimity**—total agreement.

Shelley and Robert Browning down to Tennyson and Masefield.[14] The author was Countée Cullen.[15] Or again the English critic John Drinkwater went down to a Southern seminary, one of the sort which "finishes" young white women of the South. The students sat with their wooden faces while he tried to get some response out of them. Finally he said, "Name me some of your Southern poets." They hesitated. He said finally, "I'll start out with your best. Paul Laurence Dunbar!"[16]

With the growing recognition of Negro artists in spite of the severe handicaps, one comforting thing is occurring to both white and black. They are whispering, "Here is a way out. Here is the real solution of the color problem. The recognition accorded Cullen, Hughes, Fauset, White[17] and others shows there is no real color line. Keep quiet! Don't complain! Work! All will be well!"

I will not say that already this chorus amounts to a conspiracy. Perhaps I am naturally too suspicious. But I will say that there are today a surprising number of white people who are getting great satisfaction out of these younger Negro writers because they think it is going to stop agitation of the Negro question. They say, "What is the use of your fighting and complaining; do the great thing and the reward is there." And many colored people are all too eager to follow this advice; especially those who are weary of the eternal struggle along the color line, who are afraid to fight and to whom the money of **philanthropists**[18] and the alluring publicity are subtle and deadly bribes. They say, "What is the use of fighting?

---

[14] Percy Bysshe Shelley (1792–1822), Robert Browning (1812–1889), Alfred Lord Tennyson (1809–1892), John Masefield (1878–1967)—English poets.

[15] Countée Cullen—(1903–1946), African-American poet.

[16] Paul Laurence Dunbar—(1872–1906), African-American poet.

[17] Langston Hughes (1902–1967), Jessie Redmon Fauset (1882–1961), Walter White (1893–1955)—African-American writers.

[18] **philanthropists**—those who make major gifts to charity.

Why not show simply what we deserve and let the reward come to us?"

And it is right here that the National Association for the Advancement of Colored People comes upon the field, comes with its great call to a new battle, a new fight and new things to fight before the old things are wholly won; and to say that the Beauty of Truth and Freedom which shall some day be our heritage and the heritage of all civilized men is not in our hands yet and that we ourselves must not fail to realize.

There is in New York tonight a black woman molding clay all by herself in a little bare room, because there is not a single school of sculpture in New York where she is welcome. Surely there are doors she might burst through, but when God makes a sculptor He does not always make the pushing sort of person who beats his way through doors thrust in his face. This girl is working her hands off to get out of this country so that she can get some sort of training.

There was Richard Brown. If he had been white he would have been alive today instead of dead of neglect. Many helped him when he asked but he was not the kind of boy that always asks. He was simply one who made colors sing.

There is a colored woman in Chicago who is a great musician. She thought she would like to study at Fontainebleau[19] this summer where Walter Damrosch[20] and a score of leaders of Art have an American school of music. But the application blank of this school says: "I am a white American and I apply for admission to the school."

We can go on the stage; we can be just as funny as white Americans wish us to be; we can play all the sordid parts that America likes to assign to Negroes; but for any thing else there is still small place for us.

---

[19] Fontainebleau—summer art school outside Paris sponsored by the French government.

[20] Walter Damrosch (1862–1950)—German-American conductor and composer.

And so I might go on. But let me sum up with this: Suppose the only Negro who survived some centuries hence was the Negro painted by white Americans in the novels and essays they have written. What would people in a hundred years say of black Americans? Now turn it around. Suppose you were to write a story and put in it the kind of people you know and like and imagine. You might get it published and you might not. And the "might not" is still far bigger than the "might." The white publishers catering to white folk would say, "It is not interesting"—to white folk, naturally not. They want Uncle Tom, Topsies,[21] good "darkies," and clowns. I have in my office a story with all the earmarks of truth. A young man says that he started out to write and had his stories accepted. Then he began to write about the things he knew best about, that is, about his own people. He submitted a story to a magazine which said, "We are sorry, but we cannot take it." "I sat down and revised my story, changing the color of the characters and the locale and sent it under an assumed name with a change of address and it was accepted by the same magazine that had refused it, the editor promising to take anything else I might send in provided it was good enough."

We have, to be sure, a few recognized and successful Negro artists; but they are not all those fit to survive or even a good minority. They are but the remnants of that ability and genius among us whom the accidents of education and opportunity have raised on the tidal waves of chance. We black folk are not altogether peculiar in this. After all, in the world at large, it is only the accident, the remnant, that gets the chance to make the most of itself; but if this is true of the white world it is infinitely more true of the colored world. It is not simply the great clear tenor of Roland Hayes[22] that opened the ears of America.

---

[21] Uncle Tom, Topsies—Uncle Tom and Topsy are characters from Harriet Beecher Stowe's *Uncle Tom's Cabin* (1852).

[22] Roland Hayes—(1887–1976), internationally recognized African-American singer.

We have had many voices of all kinds as fine as his and America was and is as deaf as she was for years to him. Then a foreign land heard Hayes and put its imprint on him and immediately America with all its imitative snobbery woke up. We approved Hayes because London, Paris and Berlin approved him and not simply because he was a great singer.

Thus it is the **bounden**[23] duty of black America to begin this great work of the creation of Beauty, of the preservation of Beauty, of the realization of Beauty, and we must use in this work all the methods that men have used before. And what have been the tools of the artist in times gone by? First of all, he has used the Truth—not for the sake of truth, not as a scientist seeking truth, but as one upon whom Truth eternally thrusts itself as the highest handmaid of imagination, as the one great vehicle of universal understanding. Again artists have used Goodness—goodness in all its aspects of justice, honor and right—not for sake of an ethical sanction but as the one true method of gaining sympathy and human interest.

The apostle of Beauty thus becomes the apostle of Truth and Right not by choice but by inner and outer compulsion. Free he is but his freedom is ever bounded by Truth and Justice; and slavery only dogs[24] him when he is denied the right to tell the Truth or recognize an ideal of Justice.

Thus all Art is propaganda and ever must be, despite the wailing of the purists. I stand in utter shamelessness and say that whatever art I have for writing has been used always for propaganda for gaining the right of black folk to love and enjoy. I do not care a damn for any art that is not used for propaganda. But I do care when propaganda is confined to one side while the other is stripped and silent.

---

23 **bounden**—binding.
24 dogs—closely follows.

In New York we have two plays: *White Cargo* and *Congo*. In *White Cargo* there is a fallen woman. She is black. In *Congo* the fallen woman is white. In *White Cargo* the black woman goes down further and further and in *Congo* the white woman begins with **degradation**[25] but in the end is one of the angels of the Lord.

You know the current magazine story: A young white man goes down to Central America and the most beautiful colored woman there falls in love with him. She crawls across the whole isthmus[26] to get to him. The white man says nobly, "No." He goes back to his white sweetheart in New York.

In such cases, it is not the positive propaganda of people who believe white blood divine, **infallible**[27] and holy to which I object. It is the denial of a similar right of propaganda to those who believe black blood human, lovable and inspired with new ideals for the world. White artists themselves suffer from this narrowing of their field. They cry for freedom in dealing with Negroes because they have so little freedom in dealing with whites. DuBose Heyward writes *Porgy*[28] and writes beautifully of the black Charleston underworld. But why does he do this? Because he cannot do a similar thing for the white people of Charleston, or they would drum him out of town. The only chance he had to tell the truth of pitiful human degradation was to tell it of colored people. I should not be surprised if Octavius Roy Cohen[29] had approached the *Saturday Evening Post*[30] and asked permission to write about a different kind of colored folk than the

---

[25] **degradation**—lowering in character.

[26] isthmus—strip of land connecting two larger landmasses.

[27] **infallible**—incapable of error.

[28] DuBose Heyward . . . *Porgy*—*Porgy*, a novel of African American life in Charleston, South Carolina, by DuBose Heyward (1889–1940); basis for the folk-opera *Porgy and Bess* by George and Ira Gershwin.

[29] Octavius Roy Cohen—(1891–1959), South Carolina humorist who wrote about small-town blacks.

[30] *Saturday Evening Post*—weekly magazine (1821–1969).

monstrosities he has created; but if he has, the *Post* has replied, "No. You are getting paid to write about the kind of colored people you are writing about."

In other words, the white public today demands from its artists, literary and pictorial, racial pre-judgment which deliberately distorts Truth and Justice, as far as colored races are concerned, and it will pay for no other.

On the other hand, the young and slowly growing black public still wants its prophets almost equally unfree. We are bound by all sorts of customs that have come down as second-hand soul clothes of white patrons. We are ashamed of sex and we lower our eyes when people will talk of it. Our religion holds us in superstition. Our worst side has been so shamelessly emphasized that we are denying we have or ever had a worst side. In all sorts of ways we are hemmed in and our new young artists have got to fight their way to freedom.

The ultimate judge has got to be you and you have got to build yourselves up into that wide judgment, that catholicity[31] of temper which is going to enable the artist to have his widest chance for freedom. We can afford the Truth. White folk today cannot. As it is now, we are handing everything over to a white jury. If a colored man wants to publish a book, he has got to get a white publisher and a white newspaper to say it is great; and then you and I say so. We must come to the place where the work of art when it appears is reviewed and acclaimed by our own free and **unfettered**[32] judgment. And we are going to have a real and valuable and eternal judgment only as we make ourselves free of mind, proud of body and just of soul to all men.

And then do you know what will be said? It is already saying. Just as soon as true Art emerges; just as soon as the black artist appears, someone touches the

---

[31] catholicity—broad-mindedness.

[32] **unfettered**—unrestrained.

race on the shoulder and says, "He did that because he was an American, not because he was a Negro; he was born here, he was trained here; he is not a Negro—what is a Negro anyhow? He is just human; it is the kind of thing you ought to expect."

I do not doubt that the ultimate art coming from black folk is going to be just as beautiful, and beautiful largely in the same ways, as the art that comes from white folk, or yellow, or red, but the point today is that until the art of the black folk compels recognition they will not be rated as human. And when through art they compel recognition then let the world discover if it will that their art is as new as it is old and as old as new.

I had a classmate once who did three beautiful things and died. One of them was a story of a folk who found fire and then went wandering in the gloom of night seeking again the stars they had once known and lost; suddenly out of blackness they looked up and there loomed the heavens; and what was it that they said? They raised a mighty cry: "It is the stars, it is the ancient stars, it is the young and everlasting stars!"

QUESTIONS TO CONSIDER

1. How does DuBois justify his discussion of art?

2. What tools, according to DuBois, must the African-American artist use?

3. What obligations does DuBois believe that black audiences have?

4. According to DuBois, how will black art benefit the individual black man or woman?

The Negro Artist and the Racial Mountain

BY LANGSTON HUGHES

In 1926, the same year that W. E. B. DuBois delivered his remarks on "Criteria of Negro Art," Langston Hughes (1902–1967) was also thinking about African-American artists. Unlike DuBois, who was dedicated to achieving civil rights, Hughes was interested only in the artistic expression of the African-American experience. In "The Negro Artist and the Racial Mountain," Hughes rejects imitating the white world and argues for African Americans "to express our individual dark-skinned selves."

One of the most promising of the young Negro poets said to me once, "I want to be a poet—not a Negro poet," meaning, I believe, "I want to write like a white poet"; meaning subconsciously, "I would like to be a white poet"; meaning behind that, "I would like to be white." And I was sorry the young man said that, for no great poet has ever been afraid of being himself. And I doubted then that, with his desire to run away spiritually from his race, this boy would ever be a great poet. But this is the mountain standing in the way of any true Negro art in America—this urge within the race toward whiteness, the desire to pour racial individuality into the mold of American standardization, and to be as little Negro and as much American as possible.

But let us look at the immediate background of this young poet. His family is of what I suppose one would call the Negro middle class: people who are by no means rich yet never uncomfortable nor hungry—smug, contented, respectable folk, members of the Baptist church. The father goes to work every morning. He is a chief steward at a large white club. The mother sometimes does fancy sewing or supervises parties for the rich families of the town. The children go to a mixed school. In the home they read white papers and magazines. And the mother often says, "Don't be like [racial epithet]" when the children are bad. A frequent phrase from the father is, "Look how well a white man does things." And so the word white comes to be unconsciously a symbol of all virtues. It holds for the children beauty, morality, and money. The whisper of "I want to be white" runs silently through their minds. This young poet's home is, I believe, a fairly typical home of the colored middle class. One sees immediately how difficult it would be for an artist born in such a home to interest himself in interpreting the beauty of his own people. He is never taught to see that beauty. He is taught rather not to see it, or if he does, to be ashamed of it when it is not according to Caucasian[1] patterns.

For racial culture the home of a self-styled "high-class" Negro has nothing better to offer. Instead there

---

[1] Caucasian—[anthropological term no longer in scientific use] of or pertaining to a racial group including native people of Europe, northern Africa, western Asia, and India.

will perhaps be more **aping**[2] of things white than in a less cultured or less wealthy home. The father is perhaps a doctor, lawyer, landowner, or politician. The mother may be a social worker, or a teacher, or she may do nothing and have a maid. Father is often dark but he has usually married the lightest woman he could find. The family attend a fashionable church where few really colored faces are to be found. And they themselves draw a color line. In the North they go to white theaters and white movies. And in the South they have at least two cars and house "like white folks." Nordic[3] manners, Nordic faces, Nordic hair, Nordic art (if any), and an Episcopal heaven. A very high mountain indeed for the would-be racial artist to climb in order to discover himself and his people.

But then there are the low-down folks, the so-called common element, and they are the majority—may the Lord be praised! The people who have their hip of gin on Saturday nights and are not too important to themselves or the community, or too well fed, or too learned to watch the lazy world go round. They live on Seventh Street in Washington or State Street in Chicago and they do not particularly care whether they are like white folks or anybody else. Their joy runs, bang! into ecstasy. Their religion soars to a shout. Work maybe a little today, rest a little tomorrow. Play awhile. Sing awhile. O, let's dance! These common people are not afraid of spirituals, as for a long time their more intellectual brethren were, and jazz is their child. They furnish a wealth[4] of colorful, distinctive material for any artist because they still hold their own individuality in the face of American standardizations. And perhaps these common people will give to the world its truly great Negro artist, the one who is not afraid to be himself. Whereas the better-class Negro would tell the artist what to do, the people at least

---

[2] **aping**—imitating.
[3] Nordic—like that of northern Europeans, that is, white.
[4] wealth—abundance.

let him alone when he does appear. And they are not ashamed of him—if they know he exists at all. And they accept what beauty is their own without question.

Certainly there is, for the American Negro artist who can escape the restrictions the more advanced among his own group would put upon him, a great field of unused material ready for his art. Without going outside his race, and even among the better classes with their "white" culture and conscious American manners, but still Negro enough to be different, there is sufficient matter to furnish a black artist with a lifetime of creative work. And when he chooses to touch on the relations between Negroes and whites in this country with their innumerable overtones and undertones surely, and especially for literature and the drama, there is an inexhaustible supply of themes at hand. To these the Negro artist can give his racial individuality, his heritage of rhythm and warmth, and his **incongruous**[5] humor that so often, as in the Blues, becomes ironic laughter mixed with tears. But let us look again at the mountain.

A prominent Negro clubwoman in Philadelphia paid eleven dollars to hear Raquel Meller sing Andalusian[6] popular songs. But she told me a few weeks before she would not think of going to hear "that woman," Clara Smith, a great black artist, sing Negro folksongs. And many an upper-class Negro church, even now, would not dream of employing a spiritual in its services. The drab melodies in white folks' hymnbooks are much to be preferred. "We want to worship the Lord correctly and quietly. We don't believe in 'shouting.' Let's be dull like the Nordics," they say, in effect.

The road for the serious black artist, then, who would produce a racial art is most certainly rocky and the mountain is high. Until recently he received almost

---

[5] **incongruous**—inconsistent.
[6] Andalusian—from the Andalusia region of southern Spain.

no encouragement for his work from either white or colored people. The fine novels of Chesnutt[7] go out of print with neither race noticing their passing. The quaint charm and humor of Dunbar's[8] dialect verse brought to him, in his day, largely the same kind of encouragement one would give a sideshow freak (A colored man writing poetry! How odd!) or a clown (How amusing!).

The present **vogue**[9] in things Negro, although it may do as much harm as good for the budding colored artist, has at least done this: it has brought him forcibly to the attention of his own people among whom for so long, unless the other race had noticed him beforehand, he was a prophet with little honor. I understand that Charles Gilpin[10] acted for years in Negro theaters without any special acclaim from his own, but when Broadway gave him eight curtain calls, Negroes, too, began to beat a tin pan in his honor. I know a young colored writer, a manual worker by day, who had been writing well for the colored magazines for some years, but it was not until he recently broke into the white publications and his first book was accepted by a prominent New York publisher that the "best" Negroes in his city took the trouble to discover that he lived there. Then almost immediately they decided to give a grand dinner for him. But the society ladies were careful to whisper to his mother that perhaps she'd better not come. They were not sure she would have an evening gown.

The Negro artist works against an undertow[11] of sharp criticism and misunderstanding from his own group and unintentional bribes from the whites. "Oh, be respectable, write about nice people, show how good we

---

[7] Chesnutt—Charles Chesnutt (1858–1932), early African-American fiction writer.

[8] Dunbar's—of Paul Laurence Dunbar (1872–1906), African-American poet.

[9] **vogue**—fashion; interest.

[10] Charles Gilpin—(1878–1930), African-American actor.

[11] undertow—strong current; opposition.

are," say the Negroes. "Be stereotyped, don't go too far, don't shatter our illusions about you, don't amuse us too seriously. We will pay you," say the whites. Both would have told Jean Toomer not to write *Cane*.[12] The colored people did not praise it. The white people did not buy it. Most of the colored people who did read *Cane* hate it. They are afraid of it. Although the critics gave it good reviews the public remained indifferent. Yet (excepting the work of Du Bois) *Cane* contains the finest prose written by a Negro in America. And like the singing of Robeson,[13] it is truly racial.

But in spite of the Nordicized Negro **intelligentsia**[14] and the desires of some white editors we have an honest American Negro literature already with us. Now I await the rise of the Negro theater. Our folk music, having achieved world-wide fame, offers itself to the genius of the great individual American composer who is to come. And within the next decade I expect to see the work of a growing school of colored artists who paint and model the beauty of dark faces and create with new technique the expressions of their own soul-world. And the Negro dancers who will dance like flame and the singers who will continue to carry our songs to all who listen--they will be with us in even greater numbers tomorrow.

Most of my own poems are racial in theme and treatment, derived from the life I know. In many of them I try to grasp and hold some of the meanings and rhythms of jazz. I am as sincere as I know how to be in these poems and yet after every reading I answer questions like these from my own people: Do you think Negroes should always write about Negroes? I wish you wouldn't read some of your poems to white folks. How do you find

---

[12] Jean Toomer ... *Cane*—Published in 1923, Toomer's groundbreaking literary work *Cane* was experimental in its mixture of prose and poetry and daring in its depiction of African-American life.

[13] Robeson—Paul Robeson (1896–1976), African-American singer, actor, and motion picture star.

[14] **intelligentsia**—educated classes.

anything interesting in a place like a cabaret? Why do you write about black people? You aren't black. What makes you do so many jazz poems?

But jazz to me is one of the **inherent**[15] expressions of Negro life in America; the eternal tom-tom beating in the Negro soul—the tom-tom of revolt against weariness in a white world, a world of subway trains, and work, work, work; the tom-tom of joy and laughter, and pain swallowed in a smile. Yet the Philadelphia clubwoman is ashamed to say that her race created it and she does not like me to write about it. The old subconscious "white is best" runs through her mind. Years of study under white teachers, a lifetime of white books, pictures, and papers, and white manners, morals, and Puritan standards made her dislike the spirituals. And now she turns up her nose at jazz and all its **manifestations**[16]—almost everything else distinctly racial. She doesn't care for the Winold Reiss[17] portraits of Negroes because they are "too Negro." She does not want a true picture of herself from anybody. She wants the artist to flatter her, to make the white world believe that all Negroes are as smug and as near white in soul as she wants to be. But, to my mind, it is the duty of the younger Negro artist, if he accepts any duties at all from outsiders, to change through the force of his art that old whispering "I want to be white," hidden in the aspirations of his people, to "Why should I want to be white? I am a Negro—and beautiful."

So I am ashamed for the black poet who says, "I want to be a poet, not a Negro poet," as though his own racial world were not as interesting as any other world. I am ashamed, too, for the colored artist who runs from the painting of Negro faces to the painting of sunsets

---

[15] **inherent**—inborn; ingrained.
[16] **manifestations**—signs; indications.
[17] Winold Reiss—(1886–1953), German portrait painter.

after the manner of the academicians[18] because he fears the strange un-whiteness of his own features. An artist must be free to choose what he does, certainly, but he must also never be afraid to do what he might choose.

Let the blare of Negro jazz bands and the bellowing voice of Bessie Smith[19] singing Blues penetrate the closed ears of the colored near-intellectual until they listen and perhaps understand. Let Paul Robeson singing "Water Boy," and Rudolph Fisher writing about the streets of Harlem, and Jean Toomer holding the heart of Georgia in his hands, and Aaron Douglas drawing strange black fantasies cause the smug Negro middle class to turn from their white, respectable, ordinary books and papers to catch a glimmer of their own beauty. We younger Negro artists who create now intend to express our individual dark-skinned selves without fear or shame. If white people are pleased we are glad. If they are not, it doesn't matter. We know we are beautiful. And ugly too. The tom-tom cries and the tom-tom laughs. If colored people are pleased we are glad. If they are not, their displeasure doesn't matter either. We build our temples for tomorrow, strong as we know how, and we stand on top of the mountain, free within ourselves.

---

[18] academicians—those who follow certain conventions regarding appropriate style in their paintings.

[19] Bessie Smith—(1894–1937), African-American blues singer.

QUESTIONS TO CONSIDER

1. What does Hughes see as the greatest obstacle to the Negro artist? Why does it trouble him?

2. According to Hughes, who is responsible for this obstacle?

3. What does Hughes foresee as the future of black artists?

I, Too

BY LANGSTON HUGHES

*Langston Hughes (1902–1967) wrote "I, Too" in 1925 when he
was still strongly influenced by the work of American poet Walt
Whitman. Hughes's title echoes a famous Whitman poem from
Leaves of Grass, "I Hear America Singing." In his poem Whitman
praised such common men as mechanics, carpenters, masons,
boatmen, shoemakers, and woodcutters. In "I, Too," Hughes proclaims
his kinship with white America.*

I, too, sing America.

I am the darker brother.
They send me to eat in the kitchen
When company comes,
But I laugh,
And eat well,
And grow strong.

Tomorrow,
I'll be at the table
When company comes.
Nobody'll dare
Say to me,
"Eat in the kitchen,"
Then.

Besides,
They'll see how beautiful I am
And be ashamed--

I, too, am America.

QUESTIONS TO CONSIDER

1. In what way does the speaker "sing America"?

2. What, in your opinion, does Hughes suggest by the image of eating in the kitchen?

3. How does the poem's last line vary from its first line? What added significance do you sense in the last line?

Drenched in Light

BY ZORA NEALE HURSTON

Shortly after arriving in New York in 1925, Zora Neale Hurston (1891–1973) became secretary to the white novelist Fannie Hurst and a friend of the president of Barnard College. She also became a popular and vivacious member of the Harlem literary group, attending their parties and amusing all with lively stories of growing up in Eatonville, Florida, an all-black town. She also coined the term "Negrotarian" to describe well-to-do whites who came to Harlem to befriend and mingle with blacks—not unlike the white woman in "Drenched in Light." When Alain Locke read this story, he urged Hurston to submit it to Charles S. Johnson, the African-American editor of Opportunity *magazine. Johnson published it in 1924.*

"You Isie Watts! Git 'own offen dat gate post an' rake up dis yahd!"

The little brown figure perched upon the gate post looked yearningly up the gleaming shell road that led to Orlando, and down the road that led to Sanford and shrugged her thin shoulders. This heaped kindling on Grandma Parts' already burning **ire**.[1]

---

[1] **ire**—anger.

"Lawd a-mussy!" she screamed, enraged—"Heah Joel, gimme dat wash stick. Ah'll show dat limb of Satan she kain't shake huhseff at *me*. If she ain't down by de time Ah gets dere, Ah'll break huh down in de lines" (loins).

"Aw Gran'ma, Ah see Mist' George and Jim Robinson comin' and Ah wanted to wave at 'em," the child said **petulantly**.[2]

"You jes wave dat rake at dis heah yahd, madame, else Ah'll take you down a button hole lower. You'se too 'oomanish jumpin' up in everybody's face dat pass."

This struck the child in a very sore spot for nothing pleased her so much as to sit atop of the gate post and hail the passing vehicles on their way South to Orlando, or North to Sanford. That white shell road was her great attraction. She raced up and down the stretch of it that lay before her gate like a round eyed puppy hailing glee-fully all travelers. Everybody in the country, white and colored, knew little Isis Watts, the joyful. The Robinson brothers, white cattlemen, were particularly fond of her and always extended a stirrup for her to climb up behind one of them for a short ride, or let her try to crack the long bull whips and yee whoo at the cows.

Grandma Potts went inside and Isis literally waved the rake at the "chaws" of ribbon cane that lay so boun-tifully about the yard in company with the knots and peelings, with a thick sprinkling of peanut hulls.

The herd of cattle in their envelope of gray dust came alongside and Isis dashed out to the nearest stirrup and was lifted up.

"Hello theah Snidlits, I was wonderin' wheah you was," said Jim Robinson as she snuggled down behind him in the saddle. They were almost out of the danger zone when Grandma emerged.

"You Isie-s!" she bawled.

---

[2] **petulantly**—irritably.

The child slid down on the opposite side from the house and executed a flank movement through the corn patch that brought her into the yard from behind the **privy**.[3]

"You lil' hasion you! Wheah you been?"

"Out in de back yahd" Isis lied and did a cart wheel and a few fancy steps on her way to the front again.

"If you doan git tuh dat yahd, Ah make a mommuk of you!" Isis observed that Grandma was cutting a fancy assortment of switches from peach, guana and cherry trees.

She finished the yard by raking everything under the edge of the porch and began a romp with the dogs, those lean, floppy eared, coon hounds that all country folks keep. But Grandma vetoed this also.

"Isie, you set 'own on dat porch! Uh great big 'leben yeah ole gal racin' an' rompin' lak dat—set 'own!"

Isis impatiently flung herself upon the steps.

"Git up offa dem steps, you aggavatin' limb, 'fore Ah git dem hick'ries tuh you, an' set yo' seff on a cheah."

Isis petulantly arose and sat down as violently as possible in a chair, but slid down until she all but sat upon her shoulder blades.

"Now look atcher," Grandma screamed, "Put yo' knees together, an git up offen yo' backbone! Lawd, you know dis hellion is gwine make me stomp huh insides out."

Isis sat bolt upright as if she wore a **ramrod**[4] down her back and began to whistle. Now there are certain things that Grandma Potts felt no one of this female persuasion should do—one was to sit with the knees separated, "settin' **brazen**"[5] she called it; another was whistling, another playing with boys, neither must a lady cross her legs.

---

[3] **privy**—latrine; outhouse.

[4] **ramrod**—rod for ramming, or stuffing, the charge into a rifle.

[5] **brazen**—bold; impudent.

Up she jumped from her seat to get the switches.

"So youse whistlin' in mah face, huh!" She glared till her eyes were beady and Isis bolted for safety. But the noon hour brought John Watts, the widowed father, and this excused the child from sitting for criticism.

Being the only girl in the family, of course she must wash the dishes, which she did in intervals between frolics with the dogs. She even gave Jake, the puppy, a swim in the dishpan by holding him suspended above the water that reeked of "pot likker"[6]—just high enough so that his feet would be immersed. The deluded puppy swam and swam without ever crossing the pan, much to his annoyance. Hearing Grandma she hurriedly dropped him on the floor, which he tracked up with feet wet with dishwater.

Grandma took her patching and settled down in the front room to sew. She did this every afternoon, and invariably slept in the big red rocker with her head lolled back over the back, the sewing falling from her hand.

Isis had crawled under the center table with its red plush cover with little round balls for fringe. She was lying on her back imagining herself various **personages**.[7] She wore trailing robes, golden slippers with blue bottoms. She rode white horses with flaring pink nostrils to the horizon, for she still believed that to be land's end. She was picturing herself gazing over the edge of the world into the abyss when the spool of cotton fell from Grandma's lap and rolled away under the **whatnot**.[8] Isis drew back from her contemplation of the nothingness at the horizon and glanced up at the sleeping woman. Her head had fallen far back. She breathed with a regular "snark" intake and soft "poosah" exhaust. But Isis was a visual minded child. She heard

---

[6] "pot likker"—pot liquor; the liquid left in a pot after cooking something.

[7] **personages**—important people.

[8] **whatnot**—one or more shelves, either hung on a wall or part of a freestanding piece of Victorian furniture, designed to hold a variety of items.

the snores only subconsciously but she saw a straggling beard on Grandma's chin, trembling a little with every "snark" and "poosah." They were long gray hairs curled here and there against the dark brown skin. Isis was moved with pity for her mother's mother.

"Poah Gran-ma needs a shave," she murmured, and set about it. Just then Joel, next older than Isis, entered with a can of bait.

"Come on Isie, les' we all go fishin.' The perch is bitin' fine in Blue Sink."

"Sh—sh—" cautioned his sister, "Ah got to shave Gran'ma."

"Who say so?" Joel asked, surprised.

"Nobody doan hafta tell me. Look at her chin. No ladies don't weah no whiskers if they kin help it. But Gran'ma gittin' ole an' she doan know how to shave like me."

The conference adjourned to the back porch lest Grandma wake.

"Aw, Isie, you doan know nothin' 'bout shavin' a-tall—but a *man* lak *me*—"

"Ah do so know."

"You don't not. Ah'm goin' shave her mahseff."

"Naw, you won't neither, Smarty. Ah saw her first an' thought it all up first," Isis declared, and ran to the calico covered box on the wall above the wash basin and seized her father's razor. Joel was quick and seized the mug and brush.

"Now!" Isis cried defiantly, "Ah got the razor."

"Goody, goody, goody, pussy cat, Ah got th' brush an' you can't shave 'thout lather—see! Ah know mo' than you," Joel retorted.

"Aw, who don't know dat?" Isis pretended to scorn. But seeing her progress blocked for lack of lather she compromised.

"Ah know! Les' we all shave her. You lather an' Ah shave."

This was agreeable to Joel. He made mountains of lather and anointed his own chin, and the chin of Isis and the dogs, splashed the walls and at last was persuaded to lather Grandma's chin. Not that he was **loath**[9] but he wanted his new plaything to last as long as possible.

Isis stood on one side of the chair with the razor clutched cleaver fashion. The niceties of razor-handling had passed over her head. The thing with her was to *hold* the razor—sufficient in itself.

Joel splashed on the lather in great gobs and Grandma awoke.

For one bewildered moment she stared at the grinning boy with the brush and mug but sensing another presence, she turned to behold the business face of Isis and the razor-clutching hand. Her jaw dropped and Grandma, forgetting years and rheumatism, bolted from the chair and fled the house, screaming.

"She's gone to tell papa, Isie. You didn't have no business wid his razor and he's gonna lick yo hide," Joel cried, running to replace mug and brush.

"You too, chuckle-head, you, too," retorted Isis. "You was playin' wid his brush and put it all over the dogs— Ah seen you put it on Ned an' Beulah." Isis shaved some slivers from the door jamb with the razor and replaced it in the box. Joel took his bait and pole and hurried to Blue Sink. Isis crawled under the house to brood over the whipping she knew would come. She had meant well.

But sounding brass and tinkling cymbal drew her forth. The local lodge of the Grand United Order of Odd Fellows led by a braying, thudding band, was marching in full **regalia**[10] down the road. She had forgotten the barbecue and log-rolling to be held today for the benefit of the new hall.

---

[9] **loath**—reluctant.

[10] **regalia**—adornments, such as jewelry, signifying membership in a certain order, society, military rank, and so forth.

Music to Isis meant motion. In a minute razor and whipping forgotten, she was doing a fair imitation of the Spanish dancer she had seen in a medicine show some time before. Isis' feet were gifted—she could dance most anything she saw.

Up, up went her spirits, her brown little feet doing all sorts of intricate things and her body in rhythm, hand curving above her head. But the music was growing faint. Grandma nowhere in sight. She stole out of the gate, running and dancing after the band.

Then she stopped. She couldn't dance at the carnival. Her dress was torn and dirty. She picked a long stemmed daisy and thrust it behind her ear. But the dress, no better. Oh, an idea! In the battered round topped trunk in the bedroom!

She raced back to the house, then, happier, raced down the white dusty road to the picnic grove, gorgeously clad. People laughed good naturedly at her, the band played and Isis danced because she couldn't help it. A crowd of children gather admiringly about her as she wheeled lightly about, hand on hip, flower between her teeth with the red and white fringe of the table-cloth— Grandma's new red tablecloth that she wore in lieu of a Spanish shawl—trailing in the dust. It was too **ample**[11] for her meager form, but she wore it like a gipsy. Her brown feet twinkled in and out of the fringe. Some grown people joined the children about her. The Grand Exalted Ruler rose to speak; the band was hushed, but Isis danced on, the crowd clapping their hands for her. No one listened to the Exalted one, for little by little the multitude had surrounded the brown dancer.

An automobile drove up to the Crown and halted. Two white men and a lady got out and pushed into the crowd, suppressing mirth[12] discreetly behind gloved

---

[11] **ample**—big; more than enough.
[12] suppressing mirth—holding back laughter or amusement.

hands. Isis looked up and waved them a magnificent hail and went on dancing until—

Grandma had returned to the house and missed Isis and straightway sought her at the festivities expecting to find her in her soiled dress, shoeless, gaping at the crowd, but what she saw drove her frantic. Here was her granddaughter dancing before a gaping crowd in her brand new red tablecloth, and reeking of lemon extract, for Isis had added the final touch to her costume. She *must* have perfume.

Isis saw Grandma and bolted. She heard her cry: "Mah Gawd, mah brand new table cloth Ah jus' bought f'um O'landah!" as she fled through the crowd and on into the woods.

She followed the little creek until she came to the ford in a rutty wagon road that led to Apopka and laid down on the cool grass at the roadside. The April sun was quite hot.

Misery, misery and woe settled down upon her and the child wept. She knew another whipping was in store for her.

"Oh, Ah wish Ah could die, then Gran'ma an' papa would be sorry they beat me so much. Ah b'leeve Ah'll run away an' never go home no mo'. Ah'm goin' drown mahseff in th' creek!" Her woe grew attractive.

Isis got up and waded into the water. She routed out a tiny 'gator and a huge bull frog. She splashed and sang, enjoying herself immensely. The purr of a motor struck her ear and she saw a large, powerful car jolting along the rutty road toward her. It stopped at the water's edge.

"Well, I declare, it's our little gypsy," exclaimed the man at the wheel. "What are you doing here, now?"

"Ah'm killin' mahseff," Isis declared dramatically. "Cause Gran'ma beats me too much."

There was a hearty burst of laughter from the machine.

"You'll last sometime the way you are going about it. Is this the way to Maitland? We want to go to the Park Hotel."

Isis saw no longer any reason to die. She came up out of the water, holding up the dripping fringe of the tablecloth.

"Naw, indeedy. You go to Maitlan' by the shell road—it goes by mah house—an' turn off at Lake Sebelia to the clay road that takes you right to the do'."

"Well," went on the driver, smiling **furtively**.[13] "Could you quit dying long enough to go with us?"

"Yessuh," she said thoughtfully, "Ah wanta go wid you."

The door of the car swung open. She was invited to a seat beside the driver. She had often dreamed of riding in one of these heavenly chariots but never thought she would, actually.

"Jump in then, Madame Tragedy, and show us. We lost ourselves after we left your barbecue."

During the drive Isis explained to the kind lady who smelt faintly of violets and to the indifferent men that she was really a princess. She told them about her trips to the horizon, about the trailing gowns, the gold shoes with blue bottoms—she insisted on the blue bottoms—the white charger, the time when she was Hercules and had slain numerous dragons and sundry giants. At last the car approached her gate over which stood the umbrella Chinaberry tree. The car was abreast of the gate and had all but passed when Grandma spied her glorious tablecloth lying back against the upholstery of the Packard.

"You Isie-e!" she bawled, "You lil' wretch you! Come heah *dis instunt.*"

"That's me," the child confessed, mortified, to the lady on the rear seat.

---

[13] **furtively**—slyly; sneakily.

"Oh, Sewell stop the car. This is where the child lives. I hate to give her up though."

"Do you wanta keep me?" Isis brightened.

"Oh, I wish I could, you shining little morsel. Wait, I'll try to save you a whipping this time."

She dismounted with the gaudy lemon flavored culprit and advanced to the gate where Grandma stood glowering, switches in hand.

"You're gointuh ketchit f'um yo' haid to yo' heels m'lady. Jes' come in heah."

"Why, good afternoon," she accosted the furious grandparent. "You're not going to whip this poor little thing, are you?" the lady asked in **conciliatory**[14] tones.

"Yes, Ma'am. She's de wustest lil' limb dat ever drawed bret. Jes' look at mah new table cloth, dat ain't never been washed. She done traipsed all over de woods, uh dancin' an' uh prancin' in it. She done took a razor to me t'day an' Lawd knows whut 'no'."

Isis clung to the white hand fearfully.

"Ah wuzn't gointer hurt Gran'ma, miss—Ah wuz jus' gointer shave her whiskers fuh huh 'cause she's old an' can't."

The white hand closed tightly over the little brown one that was quite soiled. She could understand a voluntary act of love even though it miscarried.

"Now, Mrs. er—er—I didn't get the name—how much did your tablecloth cost?"

"One whole big silvah dollar down at O'landah—ain't had it a week yit."

"Now here's five dollars to get another one. The little thing loves laughter. I want her to go on to the hotel and dance in that tablecloth for me. I can stand a little light today—"

"Oh, yessum, yessum." Grandma cut in, "Everything's alright, sho' she kin go, yessum."

---

14 **conciliatory**—friendly; appeasing.

The lady went on: "I want brightness and this Isis is joy itself, why she's drenched in light!"

Isis for the first time in her life, felt herself appreciated and danced up and down in an ecstasy of joy for a minute.

"Now, behave yo'seff, Isie, ovah at de hotel wid de white folks," Grandma cautioned, pride in her voice, though she strove to hide it. "Lawd, ma'am, dat gal keeps me so **frackshus**,[15] Ah doan know mah haid f'um mah feet. Ah orter comb huh haid, too, befo' she go wid you all."

"No, no, don't bother. I like her as she is. I don't think she'd like it either, being combed and scrubbed. Come on, Isis."

Feeling that Grandma had been somewhat squelched did not detract from Isis' spirit at all. She pranced over to the waiting motorcar and this time seated herself on the rear seat between the sweet, smiling lady and the rather aloof man in gray.

"Ah'm gointer stay wid you all," she said with a great deal of warmth, and snuggled up to her benefactress. "Want me tuh sing a song fuh you?"

"There, Helen, you've been adopted," said the man with a short, harsh laugh.

"Oh, I hope so, Harry." She put her arm about the red draped figure at her side and drew it close until she felt the warm puffs of the child's breath against her side. She looked hungrily ahead of her and spoke into space rather than to anyone in the car. "I want a little of her sunshine to soak into my soul. I need it."

---

[15] **frackshus**—fractious; peevish; cranky.

QUESTIONS TO CONSIDER

1. Why might conflicts between Isis and her grandmother be inevitable?

2. How is Isis's behavior typical for a child of eleven?

3. What do the white woman's final statements suggest about her?

4. What, if anything, does Hurston's use of dialect contribute to the effect of the story?

Sonnet to a Negro in Harlem

BY HELENE JOHNSON

When Helen Johnson (1907–1995) began to be recognized for her poetry, her aunt suggested she change her first name to Helene. Born in Boston, Johnson came to New York in 1926 to accept an honorable mention award in one of Opportunity *magazine's poetry contests. She became friendly with writer/anthropologist Zora Neale Hurston and had considerable success during the 1920s and 1930s in getting her work published. In "Sonnet to a Negro in Harlem," Johnson reveals her racial pride by anticipating the 1960s theme "Black is beautiful."*

You are **disdainful**[1] and magnificent—
Your perfect body and your **pompous**[2] gait,
Your dark eyes flashing solemnly with hate,
Small wonder that you are incompetent
To imitate those whom you so despise—

---

[1] **disdainful**—scornful.
[2] **pompou**s—self-important.

Your shoulders towering high above the **throng**,[3]
Your head thrown back in rich, barbaric song,
Palm trees and mangoes stretched before your eyes.
Let others toil and sweat for labor's sake
And wring from grasping hands their **meed**[4] of gold.
Why urge ahead your **supercilious**[5] feet?
Scorn will **efface**[6] each footprint that you make.
I love your laughter arrogant and bold.
You are too splendid for this city street.

---

[3] **throng**—crowd.

[4] **meed**--[archaic] reward, especially one that is well-deserved.

[5] **supercilious**—proud and scornful.

[6] **efface**—rub out; remove.

QUESTIONS TO CONSIDER

1. What words in this poem convey the appearance and personality of the title character?

2. In the context of the poem, would you describe those words as positive or negative? Why?

3. How would you describe the attitude of the speaker of this poem?

Portraits

Harlem sculptor Augusta
Savage (1892–1962) used as
her model for *Gamin* (1929)
a child she encountered
near her studio. ▶

▲
Arriving in Harlem when he was seventeen,
William Henry Johnson (1901–1970) left America
in the mid-1920s, eventually settling in Paris. He
painted this *Self Portrait* between 1921 and 1926.

▲

William H. Johnson painted
Li'l Sis in 1944.

◄ Although Sargent Claude Johnson (1887–1967)
lived in San Francisco from 1915 until his death,
his works were exhibited in New York, and he
was considered a major figure of the Harlem
Renaissance. *Mask,* shown here, was sculpted
around 1930 to 1935.

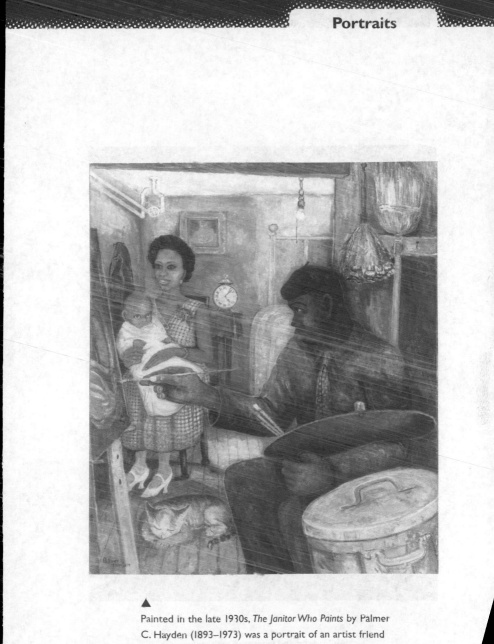

▲

Painted in the late 1930s, *The Janitor Who Paints* by Palmer
C. Hayden (1893–1973) was a portrait of an artist friend
who supported himself as a janitor. "It's sort of a protest
painting," said Hayden. "I painted it because no one called
[Cloyd] Boykin 'the artist.' They called him a janitor."

▲

An inspired and innovative artist who
won his first prize for painting at the
1928 Harmon Exhibition in New York,
Malvin Gray Johnson (1896–1934)
painted this *Self Portrait* in 1934.

Discovering Heritage

The Negro Digs Up His Past

BY ARTHUR A. SCHOMBURG

Few were more passionate about the importance of discovering and recognizing African-American heritage than Arthur A. Schomburg (1874–1938). Born in Puerto Rico to a native mother and German father, Schomburg arrived in New York in 1891, developed research skills while working for a law firm, and, later, for a group dedicated to Cuban and Puerto Rican independence. In 1911, Schomburg cofounded the Negro Society for Historical Research and personally began accumulating historical documents related to African-American history. In 1926, through a grant from the Andrew Carnegie Corporation, the New York Public Library acquired Schomburg's collection of 5,000 books, 3,000 manuscripts, and 2,000 etchings and drawings. Throughout his life, Schomburg spoke about his collection to many groups across the country, often paying for his own travel expenses. In "The Negro Digs Up His Past," written for Alain Locke's anthology The New Negro, *Schomburg stresses the importance to all Americans of discovering African-American history and culture.*

The American Negro must remake his past in order to make his future. Though it is **orthodox**[1] to think of America as the one country where it is unnecessary to have a past, what is a luxury for the nation as a whole becomes a prime social necessity for the Negro. For him, a group tradition must supply compensation for persecution, and pride of race the **antidote**[2] for prejudice. History must restore what slavery took away, for it is the social damage of slavery that the present generations must repair and offset. So among the rising democratic millions we find the Negro thinking more collectively, more retrospectively than the rest, and **apt**[3] out of the very pressure of the present to become the most enthusiastic **antiquarian**[4] of them all.

Vindicating[5] evidences of individual achievement have as a matter of fact been gathered and treasured for over a century: Abbé Gregoire's[6] liberal-minded book on Negro notables in 1808 was the pioneer effort; it has been followed at intervals by less known and often less discriminating **compendiums**[7] of exceptional men and women of African stock. But this sort of thing was on the whole pathetically over-corrective, ridiculously over-laudatory;[8] it was apologetics turned into biography. A true historical sense develops slowly and with difficulty under such circumstances. But today, even if for the ultimate purpose of group justification, history has become less a matter of argument and more a matter of record. There is the definite desire and determination to have a history, well documented, widely known at least within

---

[1] **orthodox**—commonly accepted.
[2] **antidote**—remedy.
[3] **apt**—likely.
[4] **antiquarian**—collector of old books and objects.
[5] **Vindicating**—justifying, especially against opposition.
[6] Abbé Gregoire—(1750–1831), French bishop opposed to slavery.
[7] compendiums—short, comprehensive summaries of a subject.
[8] over-laudatory—praised too highly.

race circles, and administered as a stimulating and inspiring tradition for the coming generations.

Gradually as the study of the Negro's past has come out of the **vagaries**[9] of rhetoric and propaganda and become systematic and scientific, three outstanding conclusions have been established:

First, that the Negro has been throughout the centuries of controversy an active collaborator, and often a pioneer, in the struggle for his own freedom and advancement. This is true to a degree which makes it the more surprising that it has not been recognized earlier.

Second, that by virtue of their being regarded as something "exceptional," even by friends and well-wishers, Negroes of attainment and genius have been unfairly disassociated from the group, and group credit lost accordingly.

Third, that the remote racial origins of the Negro, far from being what the race and the world have been given to understand, offer a record of credible group achievement when scientifically viewed, and more important still, that they are of vital general interest because of their bearing upon the beginnings and early development of human culture.

With such crucial truths to document and establish, an ounce of fact is worth a pound of controversy. So the Negro historian today digs under the spot where his predecessor stood and argued. Not long ago, the Public Library of Harlem housed a special exhibition of books, pamphlets, prints and old engravings, that simply said, to skeptic and believer alike, to scholar and school-child, to proud black and astonished white, "Here is the evidence." Assembled from the rapidly growing collections of the leading Negro book-collectors and research societies, there were in these cases, materials not only for the first true writing of Negro history, but for the

---

[9] **vagaries**—oddities.

rewriting of many important paragraphs of our common American history. . . .

We seem lately to have come at last to realize what the truly scientific attitude requires, and to see that the race issue has been a plague on both our historical houses, and that history cannot be properly written with either bias or counter-bias. The **blatant**[10] Caucasian racialist with his theories and assumptions of race superiority and dominance, has in turn bred his Ethiopian counterpart—the rash and rabid amateur who has glibly tried to prove half of the world's geniuses to have been Negroes and to trace the pedigree of nineteenth-century Americans from the Queen of Sheba. But fortunately today there is on both sides of a really common cause less of the sand of controversy and more of the dust of digging.

Of course, a racial motive remains—legitimately compatible with scientific method and aim. The work our race students now regard as important, they undertake very naturally to overcome in part certain handicaps of **disparagement**[11] and omission too well-known to particularize. But they do so not merely that we may not wrongfully be deprived of the spiritual nourishment of our cultural past, but also that the full story of human collaboration and interdependence may be told and realized. Especially is this likely to be the effect of the latest and most fascinating of all the attempts to open up the closed Negro past, namely the important study of African cultural origins and sources. The bigotry of civilization which is the taproot[12] of intellectual prejudice begins far back and must be corrected at its source. Fundamentally it has come about from that depreciation of Africa which has sprung up from ignorance of her true role and position in human history and the early

---

[10] **blatant**—offensively loud and obvious.

[11] **disparagement**—belittlement; discrediting.

[12] taproot—main root; source.

development of culture. The Negro has been a man without a history because he has been considered a man without a worthy culture. But a new notion of the cultural attainment and potentialities of the African stocks has recently come about, partly through the corrective influence of the more scientific study of African institutions and early cultural history, partly through growing appreciation of the skill and beauty and in many cases the historical priority of the African native crafts, and finally through the signal[13] recognition which first in France and Germany, but now very generally, the astonishing art of the African sculptures has received. Into these fascinating new vistas, with limited horizons lifting in all directions, the mind of the Negro has leapt forward faster than the slow clearings of scholarship will yet safely permit. But there is no doubt there is a field full of the most intriguing and inspiring possibilities. Already the Negro sees himself against a reclaimed background, in a perspective that will give pride and self-respect ample scope, and make history yield for him the same values that the treasured past of any people affords.

---

[13] signal—notably out of the ordinary.

QUESTIONS TO CONSIDER

1. Why does Schomburg argue for the importance of discovering heritage?

2. What assumptions do Schomburg's "three outstanding conclusions" disprove?

3. How did Schomburg explain why African Americans had no history?

The Negro Speaks of Rivers

BY LANGSTON HUGHES

*In 1920, Langston Hughes (1902–1967) was traveling to Toluca,
Mexico. As his train crossed the Mississippi River, Hughes began
"to think what that river . . . had meant to Negroes in the past. . . .
Then I remembered reading how Abraham Lincoln had [rafted] to
New Orleans, and . . . seen slavery at its worst. . . . Then I began
to think about other rivers in our past." In "ten or fifteen minutes,"
Hughes wrote this poem. He later sent it to The Crisis magazine,
where Jessie Redmon Fauset, the magazine's literary editor, wondered, "What colored person is there . . . in the United States who
writes like that and is yet unknown to us?" The Crisis published
the poem in June 1921. In simple words, sensory images, and
references to African, Middle Eastern, and American rivers, Hughes
reminds African Americans of their experiences and their heritage.*

I've known rivers:
I've known rivers ancient as the world and older than
the flow of human blood in human veins.

My soul has grown deep like the rivers.

I bathed in the Euphrates[1] when dawns were young.
I built my hut near the Congo[2] and it lulled me to sleep.
I looked upon the Nile[3] and raised the pyramids above it.
I heard the singing of the Mississippi when Abe
Lincoln went down to New Orleans, and I've seen
its muddy bosom turn all golden in the sunset.

I've known rivers:
Ancient, dusky rivers.

My soul has grown deep like rivers.

---

[1] Euphrates—river in Asia, site of one of the earliest human civilizations.
[2] Congo—river in Africa.
[3] Nile—river in Africa, site of another ancient civilization.

QUESTIONS TO CONSIDER

1. How does the speaker establish the idea of heritage?

2. Why do you think the speaker chose the four rivers
   mentioned in the poem?

3. What elements of the poem do you think made Fauset
   describe it as "dignified" when he read it?

4. What sensory images dominate the poem?

Heritage

BY GWENDOLYN BENNETT

In more than one way, Gwendolyn Bennett (1902–1981) fit W. E. B. DuBois's definition of the "talented tenth." Bennett wrote the haunting poem "Heritage" before she graduated from Pratt Institute. She taught art at Howard University in Washington, D.C., and, during the height of the Harlem Renaissance, was a columnist for and the literary editor of Opportunity, the magazine sponsored by the National Urban League. She was also an illustrator and contributor to the short-lived magazine Fire!! In "Heritage," Bennett expresses both an awareness of and pride in her heritage.

I want to see the slim palm-trees,
Pulling at the clouds
With little pointed fingers. . . .

I want to see lithe[1] Negro girls,
Etched dark against the sky
While sunset lingers.

---

[1] **lithe**—flexible; graceful.

I want to hear the silent sands,
Singing to the moon
Before the Sphinx-still face. . . .

I want to hear the chanting
Around a **heathen**[2] fire
Of a strange black race.

I want to breathe the Lotus flow'r,
Sighing to the stars
With tendrils drinking at the Nile. . . .

I want to feel the surging
Of my sad people's soul
Hidden by a minstrel-smile.

---

[2] **heathen**—belonging to a religion that does not worship the God of Judaism, Christianity, or Islam.

QUESTIONS TO CONSIDER

1. What is Bennett saying about black heritage?

2. How would you describe the speaker's tone up to the last line?

3. How does the reference in the last line to the "minstrel-smile" change the tone of the poem?

Heritage

BY COUNTEE CULLEN

*In exploring his heritage, Countee Cullen (1903–1946) uses the
challenging form of rhymed couplets. Cullen's long poem is an
acknowledgement that his African past is only part of the story.*

What is Africa to me:
Copper sun or scarlet sea,
Jungle star or jungle track,
Strong bronzed men, or regal black
Women from whose loins I sprang
When the birds of Eden sang?
*One three centuries removed
From the scenes his fathers loved,
Spicy grove, cinnamon tree,
What is Africa to me?*

So I lie, who all day long
Want no sound except the song
Sung by wild barbaric birds

Goading[1] massive jungle herds,
Juggernauts[2] of flesh that pass
Trampling tall defiant grass
Where young forest lovers lie,
Plighting troth[3] beneath the sky.
So I lie, who always hear,
Though I cram against my ear
Both my thumbs, and keep them there,
Great drums throbbing through the air.
So I lie, whose **fount**[4] of pride,
Dear distress, and joy allied,
Is my somber flesh and skin,
With the dark blood dammed within
Like great pulsing tides of wine
That, I fear, must burst the fine
Channels of the **chafing**[5] net
Where they surge and foam and fret.

Africa? A book one thumbs
Listlessly, till slumber comes.
Unremembered are her bats
Circling through the night, her cats
Crouching in the river reeds,
Stalking gentle flesh that feeds
By the river brink; no more
Does the bugle-throated roar
Cry that monarch claws have leapt
From the **scabbards**[6] where they slept.
Silver snakes that once a year

---

[1] **Goading**—prodding; inciting.

[2] **Juggernauts**—originally, huge carts supporting images of gods, whose worshipers would offer sacrifice by throwing themselves under the wheels of these carts; here, the speaker is referring to elephants.

[3] plighting troth—giving one's word or oath; promising to marry.

[4] **fount**—source.

[5] **chafing**—annoying; vexing.

[6] **scabbards**—sheaths for swords or bayonets.

Doff[7] the lovely coats you wear,
Seek no **covert**[8] in your fear
Lest a mortal eye should see;
What's your nakedness to me?
Here no **leprous**[9] flowers rear
Fierce **corollas**[10] in the air;
Here no bodies sleek and wet,
Dripping mingled rain and sweat,
Tread the savage measures of
Jungle boys and girls in love.
What is last year's snow to me,
Last year's anything? The tree
Budding yearly must forget
How its past arose or set—
Bough and blossom, flower, fruit,
Even what shy bird with mute
Wonder at her **travail**[11] there,
Meekly labored in its hair.
One three centuries removed
From the scenes his fathers loved,
Spicy grove, cinnamon tree,
What is Africa to me?

So I lie, who find no peace
Night or day, no slight release
From the **unremittent**[12] beat
Made by cruel padded feet
Walking through my body's street.
Up and down they go, and back,
Treading out a jungle track.
So I lie, who never quite

---

[7] **Doff**—remove.

[8] **covert**—hiding place.

[9] **leprous**—contaminated; infected.

[10] **corollas**—outer coverings of flower petals.

[11] **travail**—torment; suffering.

[12] **unremittent**—unceasing.

Safely sleep from rain at night—
I can never rest at all
When the rain begins to fall;
Like a soul gone mad with pain
I must match its weird refrain;
Ever must I twist and squirm,
Writhing like a baited worm,
While its primal measures drip
Through my body, crying, "Strip!
Doff this new exuberance.
Come and dance the Lover's Dance!"
In an old remembered way
Rain works on me night and day.

Quaint, outlandish heathen gods
Black men fashion out of rods,
Clay, and brittle bits of stone,
In a likeness like their own,
My conversion came high-priced;
I belong to Jesus Christ,
Preacher of humility;
Heathen gods are **naught**[13] to me.

Father, Son, and Holy Ghost,
So I make an idle boast;
Jesus of the twice-turned cheek,
Lamb of God, although I speak
With my mouth thus, in my heart
Do I play a double part.
Ever at Thy glowing altar
Must my heart grow sick and falter,
Wishing He I served were black,
Thinking then it would not lack
Precedent of pain to guide it,
Let who would or might deride it;

---

[13] **naught**—nothing.

Surely then this flesh would know
Yours had borne a kindred woe.
Lord, I fashion dark gods, too,
Daring even to give You
Dark despairing features where,
Crowned with dark rebellious hair,
Patience wavers just so much as
Mortal grief compels, while touches
Quick and hot, of anger, rise
To smitten cheek and weary eyes.
Lord, forgive me if my need
Sometimes shapes a human creed.
All day long and all night through,
One thing only must I do:
Quench my pride and cool my blood,
Lest I perish in the flood.
Lest a hidden ember set
Timber that I thought was wet
Burning like the dryest flax,
Melting like the merest wax,
Lest the grave restore its dead.
Not yet has my heart or head
In the least way realized
They and I are civilized.

QUESTIONS TO CONSIDER

1. What in the first two stanzas seems to be the speaker's attitude toward Africa?

2. What is the theme of the longer third stanza? Is it the same as the theme of the first two?

3. In what way might the stanza that begins "So I lie, who find no peace" be considered the climax or turning point of the poem?

4. What internal conflict affects the speaker from the stanza beginning "Quaint, outlandish heathen gods" to the end of the poem?

Authors

▲
James Weldon Johnson

▲
W. E. B. DuBois

▲
Langston Hughes

▲
Zora Neale Hurston

Claude McKay ▶

Countee Cullen

▲
Gwendolyn Bennett

▲
Rudolph Fisher

Nella Larsen ▶

▲
Arna Bontemps

Remembering Harlem

My City

BY JAMES WELDON JOHNSON

In 1923, when James Weldon Johnson (1871–1938) wrote "My City," he was in the third year of a ten-year term as head of the National Association for the Advancement of Colored People (NAACP). He had already been a teacher, a poet, a song lyricist, a diplomat (1906–1913), and an early civil rights organizer for the NAACP. His love for New York City is evident in the following poem, while his knowledge of its development is clear in his essay "Black Manhattan" (page 13). Considered an elder spokesperson by many of the younger Harlem Renaissance artists, he shared their enthusiasm for New York City.

When I come down to sleep death's endless night,
    The threshold of the unknown dark to cross,
    What to me then will be the keenest loss,
When this bright world blurs on my fading sight?
Will it be that no more I shall see the trees
    Or smell the flowers or hear the singing birds
    Or watch the flashing streams or patient herds?
No, I am sure it will be none of these.

But, ah! Manhattan's sights and sounds, her smells,
    Her crowds, her throbbing force, the thrill that
    comes
From being of her a part, her subtle spells,
    Her shining towers, her avenues, her slums—
    O God! the stark, unutterable pity,
To be dead, and never again behold my city!

QUESTIONS TO CONSIDER

1. What "keenest loss" does Johnson contrast to "my city"?

2. What do you think the speaker means by the phrase "subtle spells"?

3. What, if you were the poet, would be your "keenest loss"?

Parties

BY LANGSTON HUGHES

One of the most memorable Harlem party givers of the 1920s was six-foot-tall A'Lelia Walker. When A'Lelia's mother, Sarah Breedlove, was orphaned, Sarah became a washerwoman whose hair, because of stress and a poor diet, began falling out. In a dream a man appeared to her with a secret formula to overcome baldness. Beginning with only $1.50 in capital, the future Madame C. J. Walker amassed a fortune of $2 million by marketing "Madame Walker's Wonderful Hair Grower" and establishing beauty parlors that straightened hair. In the following selection from his auto-biography, The Big Sea *(1940), Hughes describes Harlem's premier hostess as well as other notable party givers of the time.*

In those days of the late 1920's, there were a great many parties, in Harlem and out, to which various members of the New Negro group were invited. These parties, when given by important Harlemites (or Carl Van Vechten)[1] were reported in full in the society pages of the Harlem press, but best in the sparkling Harlemese of

---

[1] Carl Van Vechten—(1880–1964), white novelist, critic, and photographer; early supporter of black culture.

Geraldyn Dismond who wrote for the *Interstate Tattler*. On one of Taylor Gordon's fiestas she reports as follows:

> What a crowd! All classes and colors met face to face, ultra aristocrats, Bourgeois, Communists, Park Avenuers galore, bookers, publishers, Broadway celebs, and Harlemites giving each other the once over. The social revolution was on. And yes, Lady Nancy Cunard was there all in black (she would) with 12 of her grand bracelets. . . . And was the entertainment on the up and up! Into swell dance music was injected African drums that played havoc with blood pressure. Jimmy Daniels sang his gigolo hits. Gus Simons, the Harlem crooner, made the River Stay Away From His Door and Taylor himself brought out everything from "Hot Dog" to "Bravo" when he made high C.

A'Lelia Walker was the then great Harlem party giver, although Mrs. Bernia Austin fell but little behind. And, at the Seventh Avenue apartment of Jessie Fauset[2] literary soirees with much poetry and but little to drink were the order of the day. The same was true of Lillian Alexander's, where the older intellectuals gathered.

A'Lelia Walker, however, big-hearted, night-dark, hair-straightening heiress, made no pretense at being intellectual or exclusive. At her "at homes" Negro poets and Negro number bankers mingled with downtown poets and seat-on-the-stock-exchange racketeers. Countee Cullen would be there and Witter Bynner, Muriel Draper and Nora Holt, Andy Razaf and Taylor Gordon. And a good time was had by all.

A'Lelia Walker had an apartment that held perhaps a hundred people. She would usually issue several hundred

---

[2] Fauset—Jessie Redmon Fauset (c. 1882–1961), novelist, *The Crisis* editor, and, along with others, "midwife to the Harlem Renaissance."

invitations to each party. Unless you went early there was no possible way of getting in. Her parties were as crowded as the New York subway at the rush hour—entrance, lobby, steps, hallway, and apartment a **milling**[3] crush of guests, with everybody seeming to enjoy the crowding. Once, some royal personage arrived, a Scandinavian prince, I believe, but his equerry[4] saw no way of getting him through the crowded entrance hall and into the party, so word was sent in to A'Lelia Walker that His Highness, the Prince, was waiting without. A'Lelia sent word back that she saw no way of getting His Highness in, either, nor could she herself get out through the crowd to greet him. But she offered to send refreshments downstairs to the Prince's car.

A'Lelia Walker was a gorgeous dark Amazon, in a silver turban. She had a town house in New York (also an apartment where she preferred to live) and a country mansion at Irvington-on-the-Hudson, with pipe organ programs each morning to awaken her guests gently. Her mother made a great fortune from the Madame Walker Hair Straightening Process, which had worked wonders on unruly Negro hair in the early nineteen hundreds—and which continues to work wonders today. The daughter used much of that money for fun. A'Lelia Walker was the joy-goddess of Harlem's 1920's.

She had been very much in love with her first husband, from whom she was divorced. Once at one of her parties she began to cry about him. She retired to her boudoir[5] and wept. Some of her friends went in to comfort her, and found her clutching a memento of their broken romance.

"The only thing I have left that he gave me," she sobbed, "it's all I have left of him!"

It was a gold shoehorn.

---

[3] **milling**—moving, especially in a confused manner.

[4] equerry—personal attendant.

[5] boudoir—woman's private sitting or dressing room and/or bedroom.

When A'Lelia Walker died in 1931, she had a grand funeral. It was by invitation only. But, just as for her parties, a great many more invitations had been issued than the small but exclusive Seventh Avenue funeral parlor could provide for. Hours before the funeral, the street in front of the undertaker's chapel was crowded. The doors were not opened until the cortège[6] arrived—and the cortège was late. When it came, there were almost enough family mourners, attendants, and honorary pallbearers in the procession to fill the room; as well as the representatives of the various Walker beauty parlors throughout the country. And there were still hundreds of friends outside, waving their white, engraved invitations aloft in the vain hope of entering.

Once the last honorary pallbearers had marched in, there was a great crush at the doors. Muriel Draper, Rita Romilly, Mrs. Roy Sheldon, and I were among the fortunate few who achieved an entrance.

We were startled to find De Lawd standing over A'Lelia's casket. It was a truly amazing illusion. At that time *The Green Pastures*[7] was at the height of its fame, and there stood De Lawd in the person of Rev. E. Clayton Powell, a Harlem minister, who looked exactly like Richard B. Harrison in the famous role in the play. He had the same white hair and kind face, and was later offered the part of De Lawd in the film version of the drama. Now, he stood there motionless in the dim light behind the silver casket of A'Lelia Walker.

Soft music played and it was very solemn. When we were seated and the chapel became dead silent, De Lawd said: "The Four Bon Bons will now sing."

A night club quartette that had often performed at A'Lelia's parties arose and sang for her. They sang Noel Coward's "I'll See You Again," and they swung it slightly,

---

[6] **cortège**—funeral procession.

[7] *The Green Pastures*—Pulitzer Prize-winning play written by Marc Connelly, it opened February 26, 1930, with an all-Negro cast. It was centered on a series of bible-based stories by Roark Bradford.

as she might have liked it. It was a grand funeral and very much like a party. Mrs. Mary McCleod Bethune[8] spoke in that great deep voice of hers, as only she can speak. She recalled the poor mother of A'Lelia Walker in old clothes, who had labored to bring the gift of beauty to Negro womanhood, and had taught them the care of their skin and their hair, and had built up a great business and a great fortune to the pride and glory of the Negro race—and then had given it all to her daughter, A'Lelia.

Then a poem of mine was read, "To A'Lelia." And after that the girls from the various Walker beauty shops throughout America brought their flowers and laid them on the **bier**.[9]

That was really the end of the gay times of the New Negro era in Harlem, the period that had begun to reach its end when the crash came in 1929 and the white people had much less money to spend on themselves, and practically none to spend on Negroes, for the depression brought everybody down a peg or two. And the Negroes had but few pegs to fall.

But in those pre-crash days there were parties and parties. At the novelist Jessie Fauset's parties there was always quite a different atmosphere from that at most other Harlem good-time gatherings. At Miss Fauset's, a good time was shared by talking literature and reading poetry aloud and perhaps enjoying some conversation in French. White people were seldom present there unless they were very distinguished white people, because Jessie Fauset did not feel like opening her home to mere sightseers, or faddists momentarily in love with Negro life. At her house one would usually meet editors and students, writers and social workers, and serious people who liked books and the British Museum and had perhaps been to Florence. (Italy, not Alabama.)

---

[8] Mrs. Mary McCleod Bethune—(1875–1955), African-American educator and government official.

[9] **bier**—coffin, or the movable stand supporting a coffin.

I remember, one night at her home there was a gathering in honor of Salvador de Madariaga, the Spanish diplomat and savant, which somehow became a rather self-conscious gathering, with all the Harlem writers called upon to recite their poems and speak their pieces. But afterwards, Charles S. Johnson and I invited Mr. Madariaga to Small's Paradise where we had a "ball" until the dawn came up and forced us from the club.

In those days, 409 Edgecombe, Harlem's tallest and most exclusive apartment house, was quite a party center. The Walter Whites[10] and the Aaron Douglases, among others, lived and entertained there. Walter White was a jovial and cultured host, with a sprightly mind, and an apartment overlooking the Hudson. He had the most beautiful wife in Harlem, and they were always hospitable to hungry literati like me.

At the Aaron Douglases', although he was a painter, more young writers were found than painters. Usually everybody would chip in and go dutch on the refreshments, calling down to the nearest bootlegger for a bottle of whatever it was that was drunk in those days, when labels made no difference at all in the liquid content— Scotch, bourbon, rye, and gin being the same except for coloring matter.

Arna Bontemps, poet and coming novelist, quiet and scholarly, looking like a young edition of Dr. Du Bois, was the mysterious member of the Harlem literati, in that we knew he had recently married, but none of us had ever seen his wife. All the writers wondered who she was and what she looked like. He never brought her with him to any of the parties, so she remained the mystery of the New Negro Renaissance. But I went with him once to his apartment to meet her, and found her a shy and charming girl, holding a golden baby on her lap. A year or two later there was

---

[10] Walter White—(1893–1955), executive secretary of the NAACP from 1931–1955.

another golden baby. And every time I went away to Haiti or Mexico or Europe and came back, there would be a new golden baby, each prettier than the last—so that was why the literati never saw Mrs. Bontemps.

Toward the end of the New Negro era, E. Simms Campbell came to Harlem from St. Louis, and began to try to sell cartoons to the *New Yorker*. My first memory of him is at a party at Gwendolyn Bennett's on Long Island. In the midst of the party, the young lady Mr. Campbell had brought, Constance Willis, whom he later married, began to put on her hat and coat and gloves. The hostess asked her if she was going home. She said: "No, only taking Elmer outside to straighten him out." What indiscretion he had committed at the party I never knew, perhaps flirting with some other girl, or taking a drink too many. But when we looked out, there was Constance giving Elmer an all-around talking-to on the sidewalk. And she must have straightened him out, because he was a very nice young man at parties ever after.

At the James Weldon Johnson parties and gumbo suppers, one met solid people like Clarence and Mrs. Darrow.[11] At the Dr. Alexander's, you met the upper crust Negro intellectuals like Dr. DuBois. At Wallace Thurman's,[12] you met the bohemians of both Harlem and the Village. And in the gin mills and speakeasies and night clubs between 125th and 145th, Eighth Avenue and Lenox, you met everybody from Buddy de Silva to Theodore Dreiser, Ann Pennington to the first Mrs. Eugene O'Neill. In the days when Harlem was in vogue, Amanda Randolph was at the Alhambra, Jimmy Walker was mayor of New York, and Louise sang at the old New World.

---

[11] Clarence Darrow—(1857–1938), famed American lawyer who defended many notorious criminals.

[12] Wallace Thurman—(1902–1934), poet, novelist, editor, and would-be screenwriter.

QUESTIONS TO CONSIDER

1. What does the title "Parties" suggest about Harlem in the 1920s?

2. Why do you think Hughes focuses so much attention on A'Lelia Walker?

3. What, if anything, do you think Hughes found humorous in A'Lelia Walker's funeral?

4. Why might Hughes carefully differentiate the types of guests at various parties?

5. From which of the party givers mentioned in this selection would you have most liked to receive an invitation? Why?

Conversation with Aaron Douglas

BY LESLIE COLLINS

The artist most closely associated with the Harlem Renaissance is Aaron Douglas (1899–1979). After receiving his degree in fine arts from the University of Nebraska in 1922, Douglas taught high school in Kansas City before coming to New York in 1925. Through his friendship with Dr. Charles Johnson, editor of the National Urban League magazine Opportunity, *he studied under Winold Reiss, an Austrian artist who encouraged Douglas to incorporate decorative African elements into his work. Two early commissions, a mural for a Harlem nightclub and illustrations for James Weldon Johnson's book of poetry* God's Trombones, *established his reputation. Examples of Douglas's work appear on pages 48 and 76. Here Douglas explains the Harlem Renaissance.*

COLLINS: What was the Renaissance to you? How would you define it?

DOUGLAS: It was a cultural experience; in a sense, a sort of spiritual experience. Actually it was difficult to put your hands on it, because it wasn't something that the people actually understood as *really* a thing of great importance; they had the feeling that something was going on and we acknowledged that this perhaps was something unique and destined in American black-white relationships, this touched upon the experience of black people in America, but to get hold of anything particular is difficult to realize—to achieve. So, it was only later that you had the feeling that here was something of importance to us and something that had the possibility of being a base for greater development in the future.

COLLINS: What of the man on the streets? Was he aware of anything on the way, any spiritual value being pursued by a person such as yourself, Arna Bontemps, and, earlier, James Weldon Johnson and in the Renaissance through his *God's Trombones*? Did he feel that all of you were part of a literary scheme or literary mood?

DOUGLAS: I doubt that that is true. My feeling is that the man in the street actually had no thoughts upon this thing as being a matter of importance to black and white, that it was a matter of cultural importance. As a matter of fact, if you had asked him about culture, he would have been hard-put to explain it at all, certainly to explain the black man's part in it. But he didn't understand this thing—he did not actually, consciously make a contribution; he made his contribution in an unconscious way. He was the thing on which and around which this whole idea was developed. And from that standpoint it seems to me his contribution is greater than if he had attempted consciously to make a contribution. The inner thing that came from him that some were able to understand and some of us, I believe, consciously understood (we who understand that sort of thing)—and that's the thing that made it unique, in my estimation.

COLLINS: Then the Harlemite, the man on the street, was an unconscious participant, was he not?

DOUGLAS: Yes, he was a participant. He didn't put his hands on anything. He didn't mold anything, excepting the thing was being emitted, something was coming out of him which the various artists responded to, could get hold of and make something that was later known as the Harlem Renaissance.

COLLINS: What, then, is your response to those critics who from the long view of the 60's and 70's say that those blacks who participated in the Harlem Renaissance were special beings enjoying white patronage, doll-like creatures who were manipulated and maneuvered?

DOUGLAS: To the contrary. Participants never felt like that, I do not think. Of course, I personally never felt that was true. One aspect is certain and I think we might as well acknowledge it that there were certain white people at that time that came in contact with blacks and helped make it possible for them to reach a level from which they could create, but it was *not* something dictated by white culture. It stemmed from Black culture. We were constantly working on this **innate**[1] blackness at that time that made this whole thing important and unique. And in no way do I think that we should have any feeling of being talked down to or talked into things that they had no share in, that is to say, were given certain things and were simply manipulated and so on. I think that there's no reason that idea should be maintained.

COLLINS: In your estimation, how did *The Crisis* differ from *Opportunity* as a medium for the expression of younger Black authors and artists such as yourself? You were an active participant in the Renaissance with

---

[1] **innate**—inborn; ingrained.

your sketches, with your illustrations for a number of dramatic moments such as James Weldon Johnson's *The Creation,* which through the years has been a beloved piece of literature both for its verse and illustrations. What, first of all, is your feeling about *The Crisis*?

Did it make a different kind of offer to you as an artist than *Opportunity* did? I'm thinking now that *The Crisis* was under the aegis[2] of Du Bois and *Opportunity* under the editorship of Charles S. Johnson.

DOUGLAS: Well, this idea might have emerged in other fields of art, but the field of plastic art[3] was in a unique position in that there was almost no background; we had no tradition. Everything was done . . . almost for the first time, let us say, and we were so hungry at that time for something that was specifically black that they were perfectly willing to accept almost anything. I say that because as I look back at the things that I produced, it was so readily received and cheerfully received. You wonder how they could have done it! I look at it and wonder how I could have done it. And next, could there have been a group to receive it, who were willing to receive it? And although the illustrations were definitely very primitive, very unskillful, the certain drawings that I did at that time were received and I was encouraged and I went on from that to other things.

COLLINS: Then *The Crisis* as the official journal of the NAACP was no different to you than *Opportunity* magazine was as the official organ of the Urban League?

DOUGLAS: Not really . . . They never refused anything that I did. They accepted it; they put it forward. As a matter of fact, Du Bois once carried my name on *The Crisis* as the art editor. I'm sure he had his tongue in his cheek, but he was willing to do that, you see. And I've

---

[2] aegis—direction; sponsorship.

[3] plastic art—the work of visual artists as distinct from writers and performers.

always been grateful to him for it, because it increased my motivation. I was encouraged to go on feeling that I should some day really become *worthy* of that sort of thing. My feeling was that I should go on and be worthy of the distinction that Dr. Du Bois conferred upon me.

COLLINS: Then you are saying that Dr. Du Bois *did* exert an influence on you?

DOUGLAS: In sponsorship, yes. If he hadn't done anything else, even that, what he had meant to me, for a young person reading his editorials way back when I was at an early age in the beginning of high school—beautiful things . . . the inspiration from those things was enough to make me realize the importance of any kind of association with this man.

COLLINS: Was he ever critical of you as an artist? Did he ever suggest a political angle that you might have emphasized graphically?

DOUGLAS: Yes.

COLLINS: At the beginning point of your career and earlier as a young boy spiritually and philosophically?

DOUGLAS: Yes. Yes. Tremendously.

COLLINS: Now, what about Charles S. Johnson, as editor of *Opportunity*? . . . Do you suppose he was endowed especially to help in a first step or that he was just singularly endowed with a certain kind of intuitive **ingenuity**[4] to spot talent?

DOUGLAS: I suppose the both. I suppose he was, of course, a man of broad vision. But specifically, he understood how to make the way, how to indicate the next step for many of these young people at that time and make it possible for them to go on to other things.

---

[4] **ingenuity**—cleverness.

COLLINS: In other words, he established contacts?

DOUGLAS: Yes, that's it. For instance, I met Carl Van Vechten through Charles Johnson. I met Dorothy Barnes[5] and I went on to the Barnes Foundation through Dr. Johnson. As a matter of fact, many years passed before I was out of the real influence of Dr. Johnson. . . .

COLLINS: What are your recollections of James Weldon Johnson at this time? So many of the analysts and the critics refer to him as an "elder statesman" of the Renaissance. Were you aware very deeply of his presence as an associate or as an acquaintance in this period?

DOUGLAS: Yes, naturally you knew his earlier life and his association with the stage and that sort of thing and you've read about his work with the NAACP and he had done marvelous work and was a national figure in that respect. But then this artistic aspect of it is something that was coming on. He was a man of great culture and one that was quite capable of inspiring younger men to go on in this field and to attempt to do something *worthy* of the opportunities and worthy of those who had gone before them or those who are actively engaged in this work.

COLLINS: Were you conscious of his seeming lifetime creed that the Negro had a genius, that the Black man in America possessed a genius and that he had been and was responding to that genius?

DOUGLAS: Unconsciously, I must have been. Unconsciously. I don't remember now that attitude, that idea in respect to Johnson as I was in respect to Du Bois. Yet, Johnson had been actively working in the field much more so than Du Bois, because Du Bois was a scientist. His work was in sociology, history, and so on

---

5 Dorothy Barnes—wife of Albert Barnes (1872–1951), wealthy Philadelphia art collector; patron of Douglas.

and so on, but Johnson had been actively engaged in the creative side of Negro life in the theater, in music, and so. And when he met me in the hall one day and asked me if I would . . . like to undertake some illustrations for [Johnson's book of poems *God's Trombones*], I was, of course, totally pleased. . . . And so I accepted the challenge and went on to do the sort of thing that we see, which didn't please me at the *time*. It was the best that I could do, I suppose, with the time I had, with the development I had. But I had the feeling that eventually I would be able to do something much more adequate with the material because I was and I am very much impressed with the enormous power, spiritual power that's behind Negro life and it's . . . if it can be mined, it's a gold mine if you can write or draw it. . . .

COLLINS: What was his response to your illustrations?

DOUGLAS: He was very enthusiastic about them. Apparently, it was just the sort of thing he wanted. He urged me to go on with the rest of them when I finished one of them and I went on to finish the work.

COLLINS: Well, you created a graphic phasing of the black man, did you not, that became rather a signature of yours?

DOUGLAS: Yes. There's a certain artistic pattern that I follow . . . I used the Egyptian form, that is to say, the head was in perspective in a profile flat view, the body, shoulders down to the waist turned half way, the legs were done also from the side and the feet were also done in a broad perspective. . . . The only thing that I did that was not specifically taken from the Egyptians was an eye . . . so you saw it in three dimensions. I avoided the three dimension and that's another thing that made it sort of unique artistically. . . .

COLLINS: One of the interpreters of the new impulse of the time was Dr. Alain Locke who, it is said, phrased the period the Negro Renaissance or Harlem Renaissance . . . . I was wondering if you as a young artist had come in contact with Dr. Locke and if you were aware of *his* being **cognizant**[6] of your own contributions?

DOUGLAS: Well, I think so very much. I was sort of the fair-headed boy for this reason, not because the work was, I suppose, so important (they couldn't have known that), but I was the first one to give this thing something of a Negro content. They had the feeling this isn't something that was done by a caucasian person. This is a black person. Here at last it is a black person doing this thing. He isn't criticizing his people; he isn't placing them in a situation that they would not normally *have;* he isn't trying to exalt them and you would see that in many of these things. I was very careful to associate my figures so that they looked like the working people, see. You would not confuse them with the aspiring middle-upper-class, not that I had any antagonism, but that I felt that here is the essence of this Negro thing, here among these people. So I tried to keep it there with simple devices, such as giving the clothing, any clothing, giving— sometimes giving it ragged edges, you know, so as to keep the thing realistic. . . .

COLLINS: How did Wallace Thurman organize you and Langston Hughes and Zora Neale Hurston? What did he say to you about *Fire!!* in order to get it started, in order to get you writing and drawing to produce this magazine? Both of you had no money and you knew it to be rather an adventure that in a measure became a misadventure, but did anything deter you at all? Were you always this enthusiastic?

---

[6] **cognizant**—conscious; aware.

DOUGLAS: Oh, yes. Oh certainly. We were so enthusiastic that we forgot that there was such a thing as ... these things were run with money. And that we knew what we wanted. We wanted a magazine to express our ideas, to set forth our ideas.

... Putting out a magazine was, well, just *fantastic,* I mean fantastic that we could only put out the whole of Negro life. We could only put out two magazines that I know of. Two or three. The *Messenger,* of course, the labor was so definitely behind the *Messenger.* I suppose the money that went into that was so definitely *there.* That, everybody could see. And *The Crisis, Opportunity,* but that's for the whole of Negro life,—two or three little magazines. And we, just a little bunch of us, were daring enough to come forth with a thing like that. It was outrageous, outlandish and everything else for us to do that.

COLLINS: But nevertheless stimulating.

DOUGLAS: Oh, well, certainly we thought that was the greatest thing.

COLLINS: Why *Fire!!*?

DOUGLAS: Well, I guess it was the uninhibited spirit that is behind life. I suppose that is what we meant by that. I don't remember it ever being *spelled out!* But certainly that must have been the feeling behind it. ...

COLLINS: And that experience was one of the memorable moments for you in the Harlem Renaissance?

DOUGLAS: Oh, yes. Of course, I had previously seen these things done in *Opportunity* magazine. In *The Crisis* magazine which I had been with almost a year or more. These things had come out. Some good, some serviceable, and some of them never should have been produced, but they grabbed them up and published them. As I say, I look at these things and wonder if they could have been any use to anybody, but I wasn't their editor then.

They were happy to have these things. Sure, there were other artists. There were plenty good artists, but they didn't have this feeling. . . .

COLLINS: Today, the black college student is extraordinarily fascinated by the Renaissance and its people, its time. . . . Have you any explanation for their excitement by the period?

DOUGLAS: I think so. I think they were excited because they found that at that time almost fifty years ago here were some people doing the things that they were interested in doing. That as a matter of fact their function was to pick this thing up and go on with it. We only got it started. We only lit the flame. We only set fire to this thing. But it's their business to take it, magnify it and to carry it on. I think that's the thing that excited them. And the thing that I've always tried to talk to them to infuse in them the feeling not that they were second in this thing, but it was their responsibility first to understand it—and then to take it all. The need is *greater* for them almost than it was for us in the very beginning. Their struggle and their work and their work and their achievement—it *can* be greater as we (struggle through the years) up till now. Here we are, fifty years after—being remembered is something! How many others have been remembered? But here we are. If they take this thing and go on with it, they can be *far* more . . . have a greater place in this thing than what ours was at the very beginning. That's the thing that I'll always try to make them conscious of.

QUESTIONS TO CONSIDER

1. What kind of man does the distinguished artist Douglas appear to be? In what ways does Douglas idealize the common man, the "man on the streets"?

2. What key principle initially guided Douglas in creating artistic images?

3. How, after reading this selection, would you describe the spirit of the Harlem Renaissance?

The Renaissance Reexamined

BY WARRINGTON HUDLIN

*Long after the Harlem Renaissance ended, its influence lingered
and its significance continued to be debated. In the following excerpt,
a young Warrington Hudlin (1952–   ), who directed the
documentary film* Blacks at Yale, *established the Black Filmmakers
Foundation, and became a producer of such films as* House Party
and Boomerang, *chronicles the rise and fall of the Harlem
Renaissance.*

The Renaissance can be divided into two parts;
Arna Bontemps calls them Phase I and Phase II.
Chronologically, it denotes the period of Primary Black
Propaganda (1921–24) to the eventual additional impe-
tus of white society (1924–31). The entrance of a new
directional force marked the beginning of the second
phase of the Renaissance. If this new force had a per-
sonified manifestation it would be the white literator,[1]

---

[1] literator—man of letters.

Carl Van Vechten. He did as much as, if not more than, anyone to bring the Renaissance into the public (*i.e.* white) eye.

During the first phase, however, the most outstanding supporters of the movement were *The Crisis* and *Opportunity* magazines. *The Crisis* was the official organ of the National Association for the Advancement of Colored People. W. E. B. Du Bois, its founder, served as editor. *Opportunity: A Journal of Negro Life* served a similar function for the Urban League. Charles S. Johnson was its editor. These two publications not only devoted space to exhibition and review of the work of the Harlem artist, but also held literary contests with cash prizes. The Charles Chesnutt Honorarium, offered through *The Crisis,* was a considerable distinction during this period. Their efforts did much to create literary interest in the Harlem community. They clearly destroyed the barrier that forced black writers in the past to feel as lepers, barred from print or **relegated**[2] to some obscure publishing house, many times at their own expense. It was not unusual for a writer to resort to presenting his work anonymously.

The Harlem artists, themselves, also responded to the need to develop interest in the Harlem community. Countee Cullen and Langston Hughes offered a special edition of their poetry at a drastically reduced price to come within reach of the common man's budget. This move was of considerable importance, since paperback books were not printed in the United States during this era and hard-bound books were quite expensive. . . .

The Harlem Renaissance with its black cultural revival and goal of a greater social understanding was **abdicated**[3] for a vogue.[4] The new Negro became merely

---

[2] **relegated**—assigned.

[3] **abdicated**—abandoned; forsaken.

[4] vogue—popular fashion, practice, or style.

a new stereotype. The Harlem artist could only try to raise his voice higher than the vogue [stylish] rumblings and salvage what he could.

Meanwhile, whites flocked to Harlem; some were sincere, with real appreciation of black folk-culture; others were merely curiosity seekers; still others were simply slumming. The Harlem community observed this odd procession and the hustlers in the group made some extra money.

In 1929 the stock market crashed. The effects were not immediately felt in Harlem. By 1931, however, the depression had taken its toll. One by one the artists began to leave Harlem. America had resolved to tighten its belt, leaving no room for the Harlem writers. The "good times" were over; a new environment was created that would produce a new writer in a new tradition. Many of the Harlem writers would continue to produce works, often excelling their Harlem contributions.

The legacy of the Harlem Renaissance is its art, its artists, and its idea. The reactions they encountered are for our education. The Harlem writers did not leave any "stone and mortar" institutions, but rather lived on as "living institutions." What better institution than Arna Bontemps? While the essence of the Renaissance was captured in the literature, what all this meant was **concretized**[5] in the manifestos. Alain Locke's *New Negro*, Langston Hughes's "The Negro Artist and the Racial Mountain," contemporary issues of *The Crisis* and *Opportunity* magazines, all speak to the phenomenon that was occurring in Harlem.

---

[5] **concretized**—made real or specific.

QUESTIONS TO CONSIDER

1. What external forces supported the initial phase of the Harlem Renaissance?

2. Why, in Hudlin's view, was the second phase of the Renaissance a less successful phase?

3. What does Hudlin mean by saying the Harlem writers were "living institutions"?

from

BY TONI MORRISON

Winner of the Nobel Prize in literature in 1993 as well as numerous other prizes for individual books, novelist and essayist Toni Morrison (1931–) produces works that both confound and delight readers. Her sixth novel, Jazz (1991), set in the 1920s, is the second in a trilogy that begins with Beloved (1987) and ends with Paradise (1997). In the following excerpt from Jazz, Morrison captures the exhilaration felt by many African Americans for an era that held so much promise.

I'm crazy about this City.

Daylight slants like a razor cutting the buildings in half. In the top half I see looking faces and it's not easy to tell which are people, which the work of stonemasons Below is shadow where any **blasé**[1] thing takes place: clarinets and lovemaking, fists and the voices of sorrowful women. A city like this one makes me dream tall and feel in on things. Hep.[2] It's the bright steel rocking above the

---

[1] **blasé**—uninteresting, overdone; sophisticated.

[2] Hep—[slang] a variant of *hip*; aware; with it.

shade below that does it. When I look over strips of green grass lining the river, at church steeples and into the cream-and-copper halls of apartment buildings, I'm strong. Alone, yes, but top-notch and indestructible— like the City in 1926 when all the wars are over and there will never be another one. The people down there in the shadow are happy about that. At last, at last, everything's ahead. The smart ones say so and people listening to them and reading what they write down agree: Here comes the new. Look out. There goes the sad stuff. The bad stuff. The things-nobody-could-help stuff. The way everybody was then and there. Forget that. History is over, you all, and everything's ahead at last. In halls and offices people are sitting around thinking future thoughts about projects and bridges and fast-clicking trains underneath. The A&P[3] hires a colored clerk. Big-legged women with pink kitty tongues roll money into green tubes for later on; then they laugh and put their arms around each other. Regular people corner thieves in alleys for quick **retribution**[4] and, if he is stupid and has robbed wrong, thieves corner him too. Hoodlums hand out goodies, do their best to stay interesting, and since they are being watched for excitement, they pay attention to their clothes and the carving out of insults. Nobody wants to be an emergency at Harlem Hospital but if the Negro surgeon is visiting, pride cuts down the pain. And although the hair of the first class of colored nurses was declared unseemly for the official Bellevue nurse's cap, there are thirty-five of them now—all dedicated and superb in their profession.

Nobody says it's pretty here; nobody says it's easy either. What it is is decisive, and if you pay attention to the street plans, all laid out, the City can't hurt you.

I haven't got any muscles, so I can't really be expected to defend myself. But I do know how to take precaution.

---

[3] A&P—the Atlantic and Pacific, a chain of grocery stores.

[4] **retribution**—punishment, often in repayment.

Mostly it's making sure no one knows all there is to know about me. Second, I watch everything and everyone and try to figure out their plans, their reasonings, long before they do. You have to understand what it's like, taking on a big city: I'm exposed to all sorts of ignorance and criminality. Still, this is the only life for me. I like the way the City makes people think they can do what they want and get away with it. I see them all over the place: wealthy whites, and plain ones too, pile into mansions decorated and redecorated by black women richer than they are, and both are pleased with the spectacle of the other. I've seen the eyes of black Jews, brimful of pity for everyone not themselves, graze the food stalls and the ankles of loose women, while a breeze stirs the white plumes on the helmets of the UNIA⁵ men. A colored man floats down out of the sky blowing a saxophone, and below him, in the space between two buildings, a girl talks earnestly to a man in a straw hat. He touches her lip to remove a bit of something there. Suddenly she is quiet. He tilts her chin up. They stand there. Her grip on her purse slackens and her neck makes a nice curve. The man puts his hand on the stone wall above her head. By the way his jaw moves and the turn of his head I know he has a golden tongue. The sun sneaks into the alley behind them. It makes a pretty picture on its way down.

Do what you please in the City, it is there to back and frame you no matter what you do. And what goes on on its blocks and lots and side streets is anything the strong can think of and the weak will admire. All you have to do is heed the design —the way it's laid out for you, considerate, mindful of where you want to go and what you might need tomorrow.

---

⁵ UNIA—the Universal Negro Improvement Association, an organization founded in 1914 by Marcus Garvey (1887–1940) and dedicated to racial pride, economic self-sufficiency, and the formation of an independent black nation in Africa; now regarded as a forerunner of black nationalism.

I lived a long time, maybe too much, in my own mind. People say I should come out more. Mix. I agree that I close off in places, but if you have been left standing, as I have, while your partner overstays at another appointment, or promises to give you exclusive attention after supper, but is falling asleep just as you have begun to speak—well, it can make you inhospitable if you aren't careful, the last thing I want to be.

Hospitality is gold in this City; you have to be clever to figure out how to be welcoming and defensive at the same time. When to love something and when to quit. If you don't know how, you can end up out of control or controlled by some outside thing like that hard case last winter. Word was that underneath the good times and the easy money something evil ran the streets and nothing was safe—not even the dead.

QUESTIONS TO CONSIDER

1. What is the attitude of the speaker toward the City? What effect does the City have on the speaker?

2. What specific social or economic gains by African Americans does the speaker mention?

3. How does the author link the image of light and shadow that begins the excerpt to the nature of the City?

Texts

10 From *Shimmy Shimmy Shimmy Like My Sister Kate: Looking at the Harlem Renaissance Through Poems*, edited by Nikki Giovanni. Copyright ©1996 by Nikki Giovanni. New York: Henry Holt and Company, Inc.

13 From *Black Manhattan* by James Weldon Johnson. Published by permission of Ollie Sims Okala and Sondra Kathryn Wilson.

21 "Conversation with James P. Johnson," originally published in Jazz Review (1955). Reprinted with the permission of Simon & Schuster, from *Jazz Panorama* edited by Martin T. Williams. Copyright © 1962 by Jazz Review, Inc.

27 "Jazzonia" from *Collected Poems* by Langston Hughes. Copyright © 1994 by the Estate of Langston Hughes. Reprinted by permission of Alfred A. Knopf, a Division of Random House Inc.

29 "Miss Cynthie" by Rudolph Fisher, originally in *Story Magazine*, June 1933.

56 "If We Must Die" from *Selected Poems of Claude McKay*, 1953. Reprinted by permission of The Gale Group.

58 "Strong Men" from *The Collected Poems of Sterling A. Brown*, edited by Michael S. Harper. Copyright 1932 Harcourt Brace & Company. Copyright renewed 1960 by Sterling Brown. Reprinted by permission of HarperCollins Publishers, Inc.

62 "Yet Do I Marvel" is reprinted by permission of GRM Associates, Inc. Agents for the Estate of Ida M. Cullen. From the book *Color* by Countee Cullen. Copyright © 1925 by Harper & Brothers; copyright renewed 1953 by Ida M. Cullen.

64 "A Black Man Talks of Reaping" from *Personals* by Arna Bontemps. Copyright © 1963 by Arna Bontemps. Reprinted by permission of Harold Ober Associates Incorporated.

66 "Sanctuary" by Nella Larsen from *The Sleeper Wakes* edited by Marcy Knopf.

92 "The Negro Artist and the Racial Mountain" by Langston Hughes, originally in *The Nation*, June 23, 1926. Reprinted by permission of Harold Ober Associates Incorporated.

100 "I, Too" from *Collected Poems* by Langston Hughes. Copyright © 1994 by the Estate of Langston Hughes. Reprinted by permission of Alfred A. Knopf, Inc., a Division of Random House, Inc.

102 "Drenched in Light" from *Color Struck* by Zora Neale Hurston. Used with the permission of the Estate of Zora Neale Hurston.

114 "Sonnet to a Negro in Harlem" by Helene Johnson. Reprinted by permission of Abigail McGrath.

122 Excerpts from "The Negro Digs Up His Past" by Arthur A. Schomburg is reprinted with the permission of Scribner, a Division of Simon & Schuster Inc. from *The New Negro* by Alain Locke (Atheneum Publishers, NY, 1925).

127 "The Negro Speaks of Rivers" from *Collected Poems* by Langston Hughes. Copyright © 1994 by the Estate of Langston Hughes. Reprinted by permission of Alfred A. Knopf, Inc., a Division of Random House, Inc.

129 "Heritage" by Gwendolyn B. Bennett. Reprinted with permission of the Manuscripts, Archives and Rare Books Division, Schomburg Center for Research in Black Culture, The New York Public Library, Astor, Lenox and Tilden Foundations.

131 "Heritage" is reprinted by permission of GRM Associates, Inc. Agents for the Estate of Ida M. Cullen. From *Color* by Countee Cullen. Copyright © 1925 by Harper & Brothers; copyright renewed 1953 by Ida M. Cullen.

144 "My City," copyright 1935 by James Weldon Johnson, © renewed 1963 by Grace Nail Johnson, from *Saint Peter Relates An Incident* by James Weldon Johnson. Used by permission of Viking Penguin, a division of Penguin Putnam, Inc.

146 "Parties" from *The Big Sea* by Langston Hughes. Copyright © 1940 by Langston Hughes. Copyright renewed © 1968 by Arna Bontemps and George Houston Bass. Reprinted by permission of Hill and Wang, a division of Farrar, Straus and Giroux, LLC.

154 From "Aaron Douglas Chats About the Harlem Renaissance" by Leslie Collins, Interviewer. Reprinted with permission of Fisk University Library's Black Oral History Program.

165 From "The Renaissance Re-examined" by Warrington Hudlin in *The Harlem Renaissance Remembered* edited by Arna Bontemps.

169 From *Jazz* by Toni Morrison. Reprinted by permission of International Creative Management, Inc. Copyright © 1992 by Toni Morrison.

Photos

47 Schomburg Center for Research in Black Culture. The New York Public Library. Astor, Leonard Tilden Foundation.

48 "Illustrations" by Aaron Douglas, from *God's Trombones* by James Weldon Johnson, copyright 1927 The Viking Press, Inc., renewed © 1955 by Grace Nail Johnson. Used by permission of Viking Penguin, a division of Penguin Putnam Inc.

49 *top Couple, Harlem,* 1932. James VanDerZee. Photo courtesy Donna VanDerZee. © Donna Mussenden VanDerZee.

49 *bottom* *Black Belt* by Archibald J. Motley, Jr., 1934. Chicago Historical Society.

50 James VanDerZee. The Abyssinian Babtist Church. Silver print. The James VanDerZee Collection.

74 *Talking Skull* by Meta Warrick Fuller, 1937. Reprinted by permission of The Museum of Afro-American History.

75 *Mary Turner (A Silent Protest Against Mob Violence)* by Meta Warrick Fuller, 1919. Reprinted by permission of The Museum of Afro-American History.

76 *left* *Forever Free* by Sargent Johnson, 1933. San Francisco Museum of Modern Art. Gift of Mrs. E.D. Lederman.

76 *right* *Rise, Shine for Thy Light Has Come* by Aaron Douglas, 1930. Reprinted by permission of Howard University Gallery of Art, Washington, DC.

77 *Les Fétiches* by Loïs Mailou Jones, 1938. National Museum of American Art, Washington DC/Art Resource NY.

116 Augusta Savage, *Gamin*, 1930, 16.5 x 8.5 x 7". Gift of Lorraine Lucas. Schomburg Center for Research in Black Culture, Art & Artifacts Division, The New York Public Library, Astor, Lenox and Tilden Foundations.

117 William H. Johnson, *Self Portrait*, 1921–26. National Museum of American Art, Washington DC/Art Resource, NY.

118 *top* *Li'l Sis* by William H Johnson, 1944. National Museum of American Art, Washington DC/Art Resource, NY.

118 *bottom* *Mask* by Sargent Claude Johnson, 1930–35. The Newark Museum/Art Resource, NY.

119 *The Janitor Who Paints* by Palmer Hayden, 1939. National Museum of American Art, Washington DC/Art Resource, NY.

120 *Self-Portrait* by Malvin Gray Johnson, 1934. National Museum of American Art, Washington DC/Art Resource NY.

136–137 Courtesy of the Library of Congress.

138–142 Schomburg Center for Research in Black Culture, The New York Public Library.

139 Stock Montage

Every effort has been made to secure complete rights and permissions for each selection presented herein. Updated acknowledgments, if needed, will appear in subsequent printings.

Index